*Practicing Psychotherapy*

*Doing Psychotherapy*

*Understanding Psychotherapy*

# PRACTICING PSYCHOTHERAPY

## A CASEBOOK

MICHAEL FRANZ BASCH, M.D.

BasicBooks
*A Division of* HarperCollins*Publishers*

Library of Congress Cataloging-in-Publication Data

Basch, Michael Franz.
    Practicing psychotherapy: a casebook/Michael Franz Basch.
      p.  cm.
    Includes bibliographical references and index.
    ISBN 0–465–06175–3
    1. Developmental therapy—Case studies.  I. Title  [DNLM: 1.
Psychotherapy—methods—case studies.  WM 420 B298p]
  RC489.D46B37 1992
  616.89′ 14—dc20
  DNLM/DLC
  for Library of Congress                           91–33244
                                                 CIP

*Dedicated to the memory*
*of my mother, Lilli Basch,*
*who taught me how to tell a tale;*
*and to that of my father, Martin Basch, M.D.,*
*from whom I learned what it means to be a physician*

# Contents

# Contents

# *Illustrations*

# *Acknowledgments*

This book evolved in the course of my daily work with patients, contact with my students, and discussions with interested colleagues at meetings and conferences. Though I cannot acknowledge my debt individually to everyone who has stimulated and encouraged me, I am no less grateful for the contribution each of these encounters has made toward shaping my ideas.

Although for reasons of confidentiality their names, with one exception, are not linked with specific clinical examples, several therapists have permitted me to adapt in disguised form case material from their practices that they had occasion to discuss with me. Their contributions became an integral part of my book, and I am very grateful to my wife, Carol Basch, Psy.D., and to my colleagues Joyce Gettleman, L.C.S.W., Kathleen H. Johnson, M.D., Christel E. Lembke, M.D., James P. Lynch, Psy. D., and Mary R. Schaff, M.D., for their participation in this project.

As the manuscript took form, drafts of many of the chapters were reviewed by the following members of the Faculty Seminar of the Department of Psychiatry, Rush Medical College: Robert Buchanan, M.D., Stephanie Cavanaugh, M.D., James Crawford, M.D., John Gottlieb, M.D., Peter Fink, M.D., Paul Holinger, M.D., Charles Jaffe, M.D., Karen Pierce, M.D., Gary Rosenmutter, M.D., Abbie Sivan, Ph.D., Aimee St. Pierre, M.D., Janice Swope, M.D., and Ruth Westheimer, M.D. Their suggestions were most helpful, as was their enthusiasm for the concepts I was struggling to express.

In our monthly workshop Roy R. Grinker, Jr., M.D., and Virginia Saft, M.D., saw the attempt at a first chapter and then read every draft thereafter, until the manuscript was finally sent off to the publisher. Their ideas regarding both content and form are clearly reflected in the final product, and I am more than grateful for their effort on my behalf, as well as for the steadying influence they exercised on my not always sanguine attitude to the authorial enterprise.

As the project approached completion, I asked a number of friends and colleagues to review the manuscript and give me the benefit of their critique. All responded with heartwarming good will, and I benefited greatly from the suggestions of Douglas Detrick, Ph.D., Miriam Elson, M.A., A.C.S.W., Arnold Goldberg, M.D., Constance Goldberg, M.S.W., Richard Gardiner, M.D., who also made significant improvements in many of the diagrams, Alan Kindler, M.D., David E. Morrison, M.D., and Donald L. Nathanson, M.D.

I am very grateful to Jan Fawcett, M.D., chairman of the Department of Psychiatry, Rush Medical College, who, as always, has been most supportive of my efforts in word and deed.

Many thanks to Mrs. Therese Molyneux, administrative secretary in the department of psychiatry, who has been unfailingly helpful in handling the many logistic details necessary to my work.

Once again, I take the opportunity to express my gratitude to Gilbert Levin, Ph.D., director of the Cape Cod Institute, sponsored by the Department of Psychiatry of the Albert Einstein College of Medicine, under whose auspices I have conducted many summer seminars in which the ideas brought forward in this book profited from the comments of fellow professionals from all areas of the country.

Natalie Altman, whose opinion I value so highly, gave me the benefit of her expertise when I thought the book was finished and showed me why that was not yet the case. As I expected, her telling critique made a significant difference for the better.

Jo Ann Miller, director of the behavioral science program at Basic Books, encouraged me in the idea of writing this book and gave me much good advice from beginning to end.

As you can see, I am fortunate in that there was no lack of helping hands to guide me as I inched forward. But all would have come to naught if Eva Sandberg had not been there to transform each and every revision of my written and dictated thoughts into clear typescripts. Eva and I have seen the mimeograph machine give way to the photocopier, and the typewriter to the word processor, and it is my conviction that no matter what new machinery may lie ahead, Eva and I will together be traveling that road to ever-increasing legibility.

M.F.B.

# Introduction

My purpose in writing this book is to expand, further refine, and illustrate clinically the concept of psychotherapy as applied developmental psychology—a model for practice that I first presented in *Understanding Psychotherapy: The Science Behind the Art* (1988).

As those acquainted with my previous writings know, I have a great interest in demystifying psychotherapy for beginners in the field. In my book *Doing Psychotherapy* (1980) I hoped to demonstrate that if I could be an effective psychotherapist, so could they; and from what I have heard from both students and their teachers, they have succeeded. Once shown by example that the diversity of problems brought by patients precludes a formulaic approach and that therapists can be both human and innovative, much of the fear of the unknown that too often rigidifies the newcomer to the field could be avoided. In the years since *Doing Psychotherapy* was published, I have talked to literally hundreds of therapists in workshops, conferences, and individual supervision and have found that not only the novice but also experienced, talented therapists frequently find themselves in what I see as unnecessary difficulties, often for prolonged periods of time. They are puzzled, for example, by the patient who eagerly accepts interpretations but does not change; they are frustrated by the patient who cannot be engaged in treatment in spite of his or her obvious suffering; and they find themselves paralyzed by the patient who spends the session belaboring the supposed inadequacies of the therapist, as if the latter had become the problem.

Working with therapists confronted by these and other problematic situations, I have concluded that the difficulty is not that the therapists lack either insight or empathy but that they are following a symptom-oriented approach rather than a developmental one. Our training and our literature tend to focus on the effects of patients' difficulties and the accompanying signs and symptoms—depression, anxiety, work or school inhibition, sexual impotence—rather than on the underlying developmental disturbance that first brought about the problems. Freud's discovery notwithstanding, it is too often forgotten that—unlike broken bones, heart disease, and cancer—what our patients complain of represents not the problem but, rather, an unsuccessful attempt at its resolution. Understandably, therefore, patients will not relinquish their symptoms, their crutches, until the therapists can help them walk more effectively. Looking at the patient from the perspective of the developing self lets both therapist and patient get in touch with the central issue feeding that patient's symptom.

This approach brings to mind a patient who had been seen only twice when her therapist consulted with me. The young woman sought therapy for "depression," ostensibly precipitated by the combined loss of her boyfriend, serious reverses in her career plans, and estrangement from her parents, whose side in a family feud she refused to take. The patient's therapist was bewildered as to how she might be of help. The problems were real enough, and it seemed that the patient had every reason to feel disheartened and overwhelmed. Her therapist described the patient's disconcerting habit of suddenly bursting into tears without having any accompanying affective experience that she could report. Questioned by the therapist, the patient said that these outbursts were nothing new; they went back as far as she could remember. I agreed with the therapist that in this case neither advice regarding her circumstances nor supportive hand-holding was indicated. I suggested, instead, that we think about the developmental import of her apparently contentless, tearful outbursts. Tears indicate an affective overload, and I wondered whether this patient might not be crying because she was truly at a loss for words, that is, had not learned how to relate affect to the self and then speak about those feelings.

When the therapist explored this developmental issue with her patient, the woman responded eagerly and immediately. (It reminded me of the times that I experienced a sudden loss of power in my car accompanied by a strange noise from its underside. Of course, the problem could never be duplicated when I took the car to a mechanic, whose inspection of the engine revealed nothing amiss. Since I could not be more specific about the peculiar sound, no one seemed able to help me. Finally one mechanic asked, "Does it sound like marbles rattling in a can?" "That's it," I cried, and like Rumpelstiltskin, having been named, the rest was easy.) Once the therapist broached and explained the issue of affective development, the patient recognized the missing piece and was able to mobilize and then think about her feelings as they related to the problems troubling her. And although neither ex-boyfriend, career, or parents ceased to be problematic, it was not long before the patient felt better about herself and could, as we all must, take misfortune in her stride and move on.

In this book I use clinical material from my own practice and from cases presented to me by colleagues to show how one can look behind the phenomenologic mask to identify the developmental difficulties most frequently encountered in an office-based practice, and how a therapist can either forestall or resolve those problems. These include such issues as the manner of engaging the hostile or the frightened patient; the technique for focusing a therapy that threatens to wander indefinitely and unproductively; the differential diagnosis of the patient requiring an active, hands-on approach from the one needing help to rely on introspective resources; and the importance of determining when and how to use short-term therapy.

Additionally, in chapters 6 and 7, I introduce extensive examples of the supervisory process, which demonstrate how this model for therapy can be taught and learned, and how the supervisee's skill grows as mastery of its basic concepts permits the full range of the therapist's abilities to be employed.

As always, to ensure privacy, I have thoroughly disguised the patient's history and identity in the clinical material. As I reconstructed it from notes, tapes, and memory, however, my own participation in both the therapeutic and the supervisory process has not been altered. "You make it sound too easy" is the most frequent criticism I received from colleagues whose comments I solicited while this work was still in manuscript. I have even been advised to add a disclaimer, clarifying that for didactic purposes I have made the treatment process move along more smoothly and rapidly than it actually does. I will not and cannot do so, because I have not done so. On the contrary, having heard it often enough, I am no longer surprised to hear therapists say that once *they* have grasped the method's rationale, the very next session finds the patient responding dramatically—as happened in the case just mentioned.

A word of caution: a model is not a prescription for a specific intervention; for that reason my belief in the conceptual validity of the approach I advocate does not extend to the particulars of the cases presented. The latter are meant only to illustrate principles of therapy, and I hold no brief for either my style or for any specific interventions I made. Indeed, in retrospect I can see that, given the chance to do it over again, I might say something else here, or do something different there—which only goes to show that one does not have to be on the mark 100 percent of the time to achieve respectable results, and for that, I am grateful.

# CHAPTER 1

---

## *The Developmental Model*

---

$A$LL LIFE DEPENDS on information processing. Every organism receives stimuli, converts these into meaningful signals, and uses that information to make the decisions that guide its behavior. If we look at ourselves as other animals might see us—the ant, for example—we humans must seem ludicrously inefficient. An ant colony operates as one organism: each member is geared to interpret a particular class of stimuli and to respond with sophisticated decisions governed by an inherited set of blueprints for its specialized function. Little effort is wasted, and Herculean feats are performed daily by the whole. Our evolution as social animals has, so far at least, taken a different turn. But since—with one important exception to be discussed in a moment—we neither are programmed from birth to perform specific functions nor have imprinting mechanisms that govern the details of our behavior, a great deal of our adaptive development is left to the influence of upbringing, culture, chance, and opportunity. The resulting flexibility in how we as individuals function psychologically makes for a creative potential that is unique in the animal world. But we pay a high price for it: routinely misunderstanding each other, seldom making the most of our respective abilities, unnecessarily foreclosing the contribution that each of us might make, and creating much personal suffering. Because of the differences in the ways we process information, we need psychotherapists; ants do not.

## The Primacy of Affect

Unique as each one of us is, there is one exception: an inherited program that ultimately governs our behavior. The common denominator that makes us human and holds us together is that we are born with a mobile face and a built-in information-generating program that readies us for affective responsiveness and affective communication (Tomkins 1962–63, 1981, 1987; Basch 1976; Nathanson 1987). Our affective response to stimuli remains throughout life our most important source of information and early on forms the basis for our sense of well-being or the lack of same. The affect we arouse in others is the most significant communication we can make about ourselves. Not surprisingly, as psychotherapists we are, therefore, in the business of affect management. An understanding of the nature of affect prepares us for a grasp of normal as well as abnormal psychological development and lays the foundation for a generally applicable psychotherapeutic technique.

Initially, the infant's affective experience is based on a reflex response to the intensity and form of the waves of stimuli continuously impinging on the brain (Tomkins 1962–63). Each infant has a zone of optimal stimulus intensity, and as long as stimuli fall within that zone the affect of interest is aroused. The infant's facial expression, bodily tone, eye movement, and heart rate reflect the attentiveness to such a stimulus. Excessive stimulus intensity generates the negative sequence of distress, fear, and anger—signals that the helpless infant needs to be removed from or spared such stress. The prompt resolution of stress brings a smile, an expression of pleasure; interference with positive affect or the inadequate resolution of excitement generates shame. In addition to disgust, initially a response to foul smell or taste, these affects form the basis for the psychological complexities of our lives.

Affective reactions are at first fixed physiologic responses; then at about two years of age, when reflection becomes possible, these responses are related to a concept of self and we call them feelings; and as feelings become increasingly refined and combined, we call them emotions (Basch 1983a, 1988). But no matter in which form it is experienced, affect is the gateway to action. We may think of the progressive complexities of cognitive development as being essentially in the interest of managing our affective reactions. Maturation, affective and cognitive, consists of being able to titrate our affective responses in ever more sophisticated ways, so that the all-or-none response of infancy is replaced by a much more economical investment of our effort as we sustain interest, maximize our sense of well-being, and avoid the stress of over- and understimulation (Basch 1988). As the following case illustrates, no matter how complex thought may become, it is the affective significance of what we experience or fantasy that ultimately decides how we behave.

## Anger Blocking Intimacy: George Warren

Mr. George Warren, a forty-three-year-old businessman, came into analysis for what he initially described as a sexual problem.* He was no longer attracted to his wife of twenty years and for the past five years had been carrying on a clandestine relationship with a young woman whom he found sexually gratifying. He had no wish, however, to divorce his wife; he respected her and cared for her as a person. Together they had established what was now a successful business, and they had both been very involved in raising their four children. Mr. Warren said that to leave his wife would be to turn his back on his own history; their lives were so intertwined that leaving her would be "like cutting off my right arm." But he added that it was becoming increasingly painful to lead a double life.

Once the analysis was under way, Mr. Warren described his relationship with both women in greater detail. He felt that his wife took him for granted and that it was always the task at hand that claimed her attention. He was grateful for her organized, efficient ways, which kept the household and business running smoothly, but felt she made no effort to understand him. She had no sympathy for what she called "navel-gazers." Her philosophy was that personal problems, whether caused by past or present events, were to be dealt with by immersing oneself in things that one could do something about. In what he experienced as her disregard for his needs, he recognized that she was very much like his mother. Yet strangely enough to him, he had married his wife because he considered her completely different from his mother, a

*This clinical example was used previously in Basch (in press).

3

vapid, anxious, and reclusive person, absorbed in herself and her multiple ailments, who functioned poorly and rejected his efforts to be close to her emotionally.

He vividly remembered making a commitment to his future wife, who was at that time just one of several women he was dating. One Sunday he came to her apartment to help her repair a broken dishwasher, only to find that she had already located the problem and fixed it herself. He was aware at the time of thinking that she could be a real partner, unlike his mother, who was a drag on his father. He speculated ruefully that he must have assumed his future wife's independence and efficiency implied that, unlike his mother, she could and would also be interested in and emotionally involved with him.

Mr. Warren tried to be scrupulously fair to his wife and always reminded me that the fault for his dissatisfaction in the marriage lay with him. His wife, he explained, was not a "cold fish." On the contrary, she was a more than willing sexual partner, and that, paradoxically, he found problematic. Although initially he had found her attractive and sexually exciting, almost immediately after their marriage that interest disappeared. He was able to achieve an erection and perform sexually with her only by arousing himself with fantasies of various women he knew, whom he pictured either tenderly seducing him or surprising him and overwhelming him with sexual desire. In recent years he found that, much to his wife's distress, he could perform intercourse only infrequently, perhaps once or twice a month, and then, he told me, only if he planned their coupling in such a way that within a few hours he could visit his mistress. When he and his wife were away on vacation, for example, he found himself impotent with her, though he felt sexual urges that he would release in solitary masturbation. At times like this, he dutifully forced himself to satisfy his wife's needs manually or through cunnilingus but derived no sexual pleasure from that.

His mistress, judging from his description, was a young woman with a borderline character, who depended on the stimulation of the moment for her sense of self. According to Mr. Warren, when he was with her, she focused totally on him and his needs and for a while he felt whole. Whereas he was always on guard with his wife, constantly observing himself to see if he was living up to what was expected of a mature, devoted husband, with his girlfriend he felt he could be himself without fear of being shamed. With her, he could clown around, act boyish, confess his fears, and indulge himself sexually without regard to what she might want from him—whatever he did seemed to please and satisfy her. It did not trouble him that his mistress had other lovers who, as he also did, helped to support her financially. What mattered was that when he was with her he felt she was totally devoted to him.

The increasingly detailed introspective examination of his experiences in therapy led to our recognition that anger intruded on any attempt at intimacy with his wife. The more ardent she was, the angrier he became inwardly, thinking he was being used while burying his own needs behind a facade of pseudomaturity. If he let the child within him show, he anticipated her scorn and contempt for his neediness.

As the analysis deepened and the initial positive, idealizing father transference gave way to a repetition of earlier experiences, anger came into the relationship. The fee and the limits of the appointment time, as well as my periodic absences for vacations or conferences, and any lapses in my attentiveness or cordiality toward him turned into evidence that my interest in him was a pretense similar to his behavior with his wife: I was putting on a charade to conceal my true, selfish nature.

Through the interpretation of the negative mother transference it became possible to link his anger to his mother's seeming inability to respond to his needs earlier in his life. Eventually, as he grew able to separate mother from wife, his emotional and sexual relationship with his wife became much more satisfying to him.

Although played out in the sexual arena, there was never any question of decreased sexual desire in this patient. It was the difference in the unconscious affective reactions to his wife and mistress respectively that was crucial and that governed Mr. Warren's sexual behavior with each of these women. His improvement is explained by the fact that once analysis resolved the patient's negative mother transference toward his wife, his feelings about her were significantly altered, allowing his wife, among other things, to become an object of his sexual interest.*

---

*It should be added that I considered Mr. Warren to have a problem in attachment rather than a psychosexual conflict. This differentiation will be discussed shortly (pp. 22–24).

## The Search for Competence

As I have discussed in detail elsewhere (Basch 1988), from infancy on we learn to set goals and strive to achieve them. This search for competence forms the basis for healthy psychological development and a sense of a cohesive, functioning self. Attaining competence in a given situation results in a state of well-being, which we call self-esteem.

In everyday usage, *competence* usually refers only to the ability to perform; that is not how I am using the word here. The great investigator of cognitive psychology, Jean Piaget (Piaget and Inhelder 1969), spoke of two aspects of functional maturation: *accommodation*—the effective adaptation to the environment—and *assimilation*—the capacity to mold external reality to one's needs. *Competence,* as I use the term, encompasses both accommodation and assimilation, or satisfactory affect management. In this sense, the reason, whether they know it or not, that people come to the attention of a psychotherapist is that they judge themselves, or are judged to be, less than competent in some significant respect: that is, they are unable to function reasonably well in their environment and/or are insufficiently affectively rewarded by their adaptation to their situation. Our job as therapists is to promote and/or restore, insofar as it is possible, the patient's capacity to set reasonable goals and strive for their fulfillment. The following paradigmatic case vignette will illustrate what I mean.

## Restoring a Patient's Self-Esteem: Harriet Snow

Harriet Snow, a forty-year-old, unmarried, successful commercial photographer, was hospitalized in the terminal stages of cancer. The patient knew the nature of her condition and its hopeless prognosis. She was being kept alive only by heroic, but often painful measures. One day she asked her nurse, "Do you think I will die soon?" The nurse, obviously upset by the question, did not answer her; she turned on her heel, ran out of the room, and reported the incident to her supervisor. A psychiatric consultation was then sought for the patient to establish whether Miss Snow was suicidal.

The resident in psychiatry who responded to the consultation request first informed herself of the patient's medical condition and the incident leading to the consultation. Then, introducing herself, she sat down with Miss Snow and asked what was on her mind when she questioned the nurse—had her condition become so painful that she was planning to end her life? Miss Snow said that the agony of her illness, compounded by the procedures keeping her alive, made her long for death, but far from planning suicide, she felt she owed it to her father to stay alive. She said that he was so devastated by the thought of losing her that he had urged the doctors to do everything to prolong her life; she felt she had no choice but to comply.

The psychiatrist asked if her father was aware of how much she suffered. Miss Snow said that every time she saw him, her father was tearful, upset, and clearly bent on avoiding any substantive discussion of her condition. She could not bring herself to discuss frankly either what both knew to be her fate or what she was enduring.

Miss Snow then spontaneously began to talk about her family: the death of her mother a few years ago and the close relationship that had developed between her, an only child, and her father, whose profession she shared.

At the close of their first encounter, the psychiatrist offered to talk to her father for her or to mediate a meeting between the two of them. Although grateful for the offer, Miss Snow said she now felt she could talk to her father alone. Thus, for the first time, the two of them faced the inevitable together. After their talk they spoke to her physician and asked that he and the staff do no more than make her comfortable in her last days.

The psychiatrist continued to see Miss Snow daily. They talked about such issues as the decisions confronting the patient between her need to take sufficient drugs to relieve her pain and her wish to remain as mentally alert as possible. With the psychiatrist's encouragement, Miss Snow was able to plan and say her goodbyes to people who mattered to her. She went through some mourning for her formerly active life and, shyly but with pride, showed the psychiatrist the photographs she had taken for various publications. Clearly pleased by the therapist's genuine admiration for her work, she engaged with surprising vitality in a conversation about her training and her art.

Shortly before she sank into the coma that marked the end of her life,

Miss Snow expressed her appreciation to the psychiatrist. The latter replied, "And you too have contributed something important to *my* life; I learned much from you, and our working together meant a great deal to me also." The patient's face brightened; she was obviously deeply moved.

I give this vignette not simply because it is a touching story and an exemplary piece of work with a dying patient, but because it encapsulates the essence of psychotherapy—doing what is needed to enable the patient to achieve or regain competence and the sense of control and self-esteem that accompanies it. When Miss Snow was first seen, she believed that she had no control over her life and could no longer influence her destiny. Her question about when she would die was not signaling movement toward the resolution of her agonizing situation but, rather, a retreating to withdrawal, the developmentally earliest defense available against excessive negative affect (Basch 1988). Like a baby who goes to sleep when things are beyond its capacity to manage or tolerate, Miss Snow wanted only to escape what had become too painful and meaningless.

Without the exercise of control, there is neither interest nor pleasure; Miss Snow experienced only distress and the expectation of pain. She acted as if she were a passive victim of her environment, an environment that had implicitly labeled her helpless because she was dying, and her behavior indicated that she had accepted that designation. Miss Snow believed that her illness, coupled with her father's needs, precluded her from any initiative that would lead to competence and self-assertion. With the therapist's help, Miss Snow regained the confidence to see herself as a person capable of having desires and implementing her decisions. She found herself interested and interesting, and even though death was imminent, she regained her self-esteem: she became once again a competent, self-respecting person.

Our patients often come to us with the belief that what they need, and are looking for, is happiness, by which they usually mean a problem-free existence, or at least an existence free from the problems confronting them. But that wish is not in our power to grant, nor is it a goal we need to strive for. Miss Snow was certainly neither problem-free nor happy as the result of her treatment, yet it was very rewarding for her. When successful, we as therapists help our patients to learn and accept what it is *they* must do to establish or reestablish competence and a healthy self-esteem. The achievement is and must be the patient's; we do what we can to remove obstacles in the path of their efforts in that direction.

Competence and self-esteem are not to be confused with worldly success. We see many patients who have made their mark as executives, professionals, or homemakers, but who are sufficiently miserable with their lot to seek help, puzzled all the while that they are not contented when they have achieved what most people only dream about. As these patients show, though such accomplishments are not barriers to happiness, they cannot be equated with it either. During my time in the service it was a maxim that when consulting in the hospital with a patient who was a general, an admiral, or other high-ranking officer, one had to make sure he or she was not in uniform during the interview, lest we junior officers become blinded by such achievement and unable to empathize with the patient's difficulties: how could someone so successful, powerful, and important have problems?

I recall one touching case in which a rear admiral being considered for promotion suffered a stress reaction and came for consultation because he did not know whether to accept this honor or retire and fulfill his dream of becoming a race car mechanic. A race car mechanic as opposed to a vice-admiral? I am afraid I was too young, too inexperienced, and, most important, not in possession of an appropriate theoretical framework with which to understand his dilemma. Today, faced with such a situation, I would be quite comfortable investigating with this patient how he attained his present position and why this superior accommodation fell short of the assimilation or personal satisfaction to make him reasonably interested and content. It might well turn out, as it has in many cases, that the initial complaint or problem was not the basic issue with which the patient had to deal, but one has to start somewhere.

I apply in my practice and emphasize in my teaching that we as therapists have to establish a focus for the session and ultimately for the therapy. We are certainly guided by the patient's fluctuating needs and interests, but with few exceptions (see the case of Mrs. Pellman, pp. 20–24) we must function as guides to let our work with a particular patient achieve cohesion and prevent drifting. I advocate that, keeping the concept of striving for competence—assimilation and accommodation—in mind, we evaluate what the patient is saying in these terms and then question, clarify, explain, and interpret accordingly.

## The Developmental Spiral

Miss Snow, who had been a highly competent individual, lost that competence and the healthy self-esteem that goes with it when she acquiesced to the implicit role assigned to her as a terminally ill person. She found herself treated as if she no longer had the right or ability to make decisions. Beginning with the initial interview, her psychiatrist reversed that destructive assumption by treating Miss Snow with the courtesy and respect normally accorded healthy people: that is, she treated Miss Snow as a decision maker—had Miss Snow decided to end her life? The patient said she had not and explained her situation. From that point on, her psychological improvement was dramatic and Miss Snow began to behave in ways that restored her self-esteem. She lived out her last weeks with self-respect and died with dignity.

This case illustrates what I have elsewhere (1988) called the developmental spiral (see figure 1.1). As the diagram illustrates, the basis of what we call our mind or mental life are the goal-directed decisions we make and then implement. If our behavior proves competent, it enhances our sense of well-being or self-esteem, providing an experience that serves as the basis for future decisions and behavior. This spiraling and expanding process is what we call maturation.

As we all know too well, maturation is not by any means an uninterrupted triumphal march. We make decisions that turn out to be erroneous; even when correct, the behavior employed to implement our decisions often is inadequate or faulty; the self-esteem that is rightfully ours is spoiled by some disappointment that attends our very success, and so on. But that is not pathology; that is life.

As long as the quest for competence continues and our failure to achieve it at a particular time or in a given area informs our attempts at correction, we are in good balance. Perhaps that dynamic equilibrium is as good a description of mental health as any that I can think of. The kind of problem with which we as psychotherapists concern ourselves begins when experience ceases to be informative, when it ceases to lead to new and, one hopes, more effective decision making. When the information-processing system we call our mind shuts down and, in one or more significant areas, is caught in a vicious cycle, a self-fulfilling prophecy occurs in which decisions that have proven counterproductive continue to be made essentially unaltered. A downward or pathological

The Developmental Model

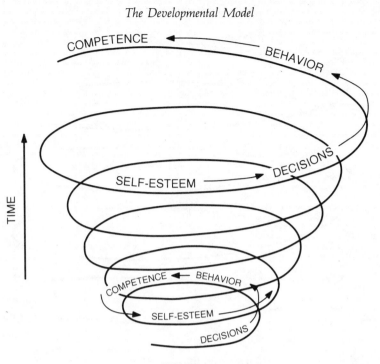

FIGURE 1.1
The Developmental Spiral

Reprinted by permission from Michael Franz Basch, *Understanding Psychotherapy* (Basic Books, 1988, p. 29).

spiral is perpetuated, (figure 1.2) generating the situations and syndromes that lead people to seek psychotherapeutic help.

No matter what the problem may be that the patient presents, we as therapists aim to identify and help the patient to reverse the pathological spiral and restore the appropriate developmental one. We then determine where the pathological spiral offers the best opportunity for intervention. Shall we investigate the patients' decisions that seem to have created the problem? Should we examine their behavior? Focus on the question of competence? Or should we emphasize self-esteem issues?

Sooner or later in an ongoing therapy one will, of course, touch on all of these questions, but where does one begin? As we review the therapist's approach to Miss Snow, we see that by her very attitude toward the patient the therapist addressed the issue of self-esteem. Treating Miss Snow with the respect due another human being reversed

11

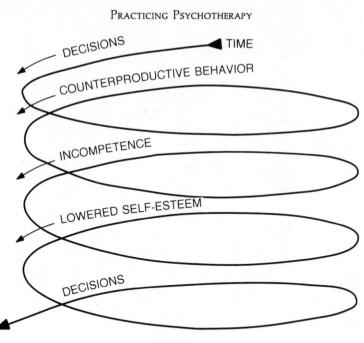

FIGURE 1.2
The Pathological Spiral

the downward course and let the patient resume making reasonable decisions about her life. In retrospect, in the case of the admiral who consulted me, I now think I would enter the spiral at the decision-making level—how did he decide to go into the navy rather than to become a race car mechanic? That approach, I think, would have led to a meaningful unfolding of his life history, out of which some answers to his dilemma could emerge. As further clinical examples will show, I have found it helpful to think about possible interventions that I might make in terms of the developmental spiral and the course from decision making to self-esteem.

## The Evaluation of Competence

As important as ascertaining what is "wrong" with the patient is learning what is "right" with that patient. What, developmentally speaking, are the patient's strengths? The patient's developmental assets and potential for growth afford the therapist the leverage needed to engage the patient and help that patient attain competence in those areas where maturation has lagged or is threatened.

## Building Psychic Structure: Roberta Young

Roberta, three and a half years old, was referred for therapy by the family's social worker. Roberta had been severely abused by her mother; her father's whereabouts were unknown. A court order had placed Roberta in a foster home when the child was two years old. Her foster mother, a kind but somewhat rigid older woman, complained to the social worker that Roberta was hard to manage. For the most part uncommunicative, Roberta was given to sudden, violent outbursts, and, even at her best, behaved in a disorganized manner that disrupted the household.

When the therapist first saw Roberta in the waiting room with her foster mother, the child appeared well groomed. She was a pretty little girl who sat passively with a depressed expression on her face.

THERAPIST: Hi, Roberta, I'm Liz *(extends her hand to the child, who ignores it)*. We are going to talk and play together. We have our special time every week, just you and I, and mother will wait out here for you. *(Turning to mother)* Will you be waiting here for us throughout the session? *(Mother nods assent.)* Okay, Roberta, shall we go now? *(Roberta has said nothing so far, but nods silently, gets up, and goes with the therapist to the office.)*

In the office/playroom, Roberta stood quietly looking around. Her facial expression was one of apprehension, but she seemed to take in the entire room.

ROBERTA: *(Walks over to a closet, opens the door, goes half-way in, and abruptly turns to the therapist.)* Don't you close that door on me!
THERAPIST: Of course I wouldn't do that, Roberta. I would never shut you up in a closet. *(Roberta, having looked around the closet, backs out and starts wandering through the rest of the room. She sees a box of building blocks and, saying nothing, walks over to it and dumps its contents on the floor.)* Oh, we're going to build with blocks. I like

blocks. May I join you? *(The therapist has decided to enter the developmental spiral at the behavioral level. Roberta says nothing, and the therapist sits down across from Roberta. Roberta listlessly lines up six square blocks in a long, wavy line, and then haphazardly piles six blocks on top.)* Looks like you're building a house? *(Roberta nods.)* Can I build a house too? *(Roberta nods her head yes and continues building up her wall of blocks.)* I like your house, Roberta. *(Therapist continues to build the house that she is working on.)* I think I'll just put a smokestack on mine. *(Picks up a cylindrical block and places it on top of the "house." Having finished her house, the therapist indicates that she has finished her project by extending both arms horizontally in a dramatic gesture.)* Ta-da! All done, Roberta. *(Roberta then finishes her "house" and places a cylindrical "smokestack" on top, just as the therapist had done.)*

THERAPIST: Oh, great! *(She claps her hands in approval and congratulation.)*

ROBERTA: *(When she first hears the therapist clapping, she flinches, as if she is about to be hit, and then looks astonished. Roberta then starts to build a new structure; the blocks are much less strung out and placed more tightly together, giving it a more solid appearance than her first "house" had.)*

THERAPIST: *(Watching quietly while Roberta is building, eventually says)* Oh, we're going to have a regular neighborhood, a whole bunch of houses.

ROBERTA: *(Completes her house, puts a smokestack on by herself, looks at the therapist, and smiles for the first time. She then extends her arms, as the therapist had done, and, with the same triumphant tone says, "Ta-da!" and claps for herself, the therapist joining in. Roberta then goes to another corner of the room, fetches a doll and, although her words are not very clear, is obviously teaching the doll how to build a house.)*

At the end of the session, the therapist walks out with Roberta who, finding her foster mother sitting in the waiting room, runs over to her with an animated expression on her face.

ROBERTA: Me and Liz builded houses! *(She is about to extend her arms as before, but checks herself and smiles a little sheepishly.)*

THERAPIST: Oh, Roberta was great. We had a good time and we'll see you again next week. *(Extends her hand to Roberta, who, this time, takes it.)* See you soon, Roberta.

What is encouraging about the first clinical encounter with Roberta is that in spite of her initially isolated and suspicious attitude, she was able to accept the opportunity to make contact with the therapist and then demonstrate a flowering of affect and increasingly complex competent behavior. Analyzing what the therapist did in terms of the developmental spiral, I would say that she implicitly understood that Roberta's past experience had probably not allowed the child to build a healthy self-esteem by making and implementing age-appropriate decisions. The therapist then took every opportunity to support Roberta's initiatives: For example, the therapist reassured Roberta that she was safe in her decision to explore the closet; she encouraged Roberta's decision to play with blocks, and then used that opportunity to let the child experience increasingly competent performance and the self-esteem that comes with achievement. Where there had been only muted distress and the anticipation of pain, now there was interest, joy, and healthy excitement. One gets the impression that, though Roberta's history and initial behavior indicate serious problems, there is still a great deal of potential for healthy development, which can be turned to therapeutic use.

# CHAPTER 2

---

## The Hierarchy of Selfobject Experiences

---

O BVIOUSLY, ON THE BASIS of her first session we cannot come to any conclusions about the course or results of Roberta's therapy, but what happened in that first session was certainly surprising and positive. Roberta's dramatic change in behavior during her treatment session was made possible by her ability to use the therapist to generate what the psychoanalyst Heinz Kohut has called "selfobject experiences." Kohut (1971, 1977, 1984) systematically investigated and applied clinically what now, in retrospect, seems only obvious and sensible: namely, that throughout life, when our ability to cope effectively threatens our psychological integrity, we need assistance and support in order to keep our balance and move on. Kohut coined the term *selfobject relationship*, or *selfobject experience*, contrasting it to "object relationship." He wanted to indicate that in selfobject situations the person is focused on his or her own self, more or less exclusively, and is for practical purposes oblivious to the existence and needs of the other person, that is, of the other's or "object's" existence and needs. Kohut (1984) divided selfobject experiences into three types, based on the service rendered to the endangered self: mirroring, idealizing, and alter ego or twinship.

My clinical experience leads me to agree with Douglas Detrick (1986) that the most basic of these three is the alter ego or twinship experience. I prefer to call this the "kinship experience" because it asserts and strengthens the sense of being a member of a group—the acceptance that comes from "being like" the other. It is the appreciation of, and

17

resonance with, another's affect that is probably the most important factor in promoting a kinship experience. (It is my opinion that much of what Kohut [1971] called the merger aspect of the mirror transference is actually the earliest form of the need for kinship; that is, the infant's need to have communicated through the parents' ministrations and responsiveness that he or she is accepted as one of, and with, them.)

Knowing that one is not at the mercy of one's immaturity and inadequacy but can draw on the wisdom and power of benign others gives rise to Kohut's "idealizing" selfobject experience, a trusting dependence.

And, finally, the strength that comes from being understood by others who show through attitudes, words, and/or actions that they resonate with one's experience generates Kohut's "mirroring" or, as I prefer to call it, "validating" selfobject experiences.

People who need our psychotherapeutic services are fundamentally hampered in their search for competence, that is, have a significantly damaged self and are therefore in need of selfobject experiences that will permit them to continue their search in a more satisfactory manner. The question then is whether the patient can use the therapist to generate appropriate selfobject experiences, or whether past painful disappointments have led that patient to seal off the area in question—in technical terms, led him to defend himself against transferring his needs to the therapist. In Roberta's case we saw that, fortunately, she had not shut herself off and was able to use the therapist to remobilize her needs for a healthy, probably maternal attachment. Indeed, Roberta's session repeated in the microcosm of the hour the three selfobject needs of which Kohut wrote: the kinship experience began when the therapist, in introducing herself and setting the stage for their meeting, oriented Roberta to what would happen in the session, assuring her of the continuity of their relationship ("We have our special time every week."). The therapist's treating Roberta as she (the therapist) would want to be treated upon facing a new, strange situation conveys the assumption that she and Roberta share a fundamental similarity.

She continued to assure Roberta of kinship by rejecting the very notion that, as Roberta feared, she might shut the closet door on her. Roberta gave evidence that she could accept the therapist's acceptance, so to speak, when she let the therapist join her in a game. An indicator that Roberta had moved on to an idealizing selfobject experience—that she had drawn strength and direction from the therapist—came when her desultory arrangement of the building blocks was replaced by genuine interest and the building of a "house" similar to the one the therapist had constructed. Proof that the therapist's approval of Roberta's effort, a mirroring or validating of Roberta's performance, had succeeded was shown when Roberta, using the therapist's mannerisms, expressed joy and pride in her own achievement. Having been validated, Roberta was now free to validate herself.

Those familiar with the work of Heinz Kohut and the literature that has grown up around it contend that he regards the needs for kinship, idealization, and mirroring as independently existing needs and/or transferences, but I do not believe that this is the case. In my clinical experience, kinship, idealization, and mirroring form a continuum in which the sense of kinship is basic to the emergence of idealization and, in turn, the capacity for idealization is a prerequisite for the fulfillment of the need for mirroring (figure 2.1).

As I have said, a kinship relation between therapist and patient is essential for therapy to take place. But given that basis, it is the idealizing transference that then enables the therapy to progress. The patient's belief, usually unconscious, that the therapist—like the parent he had or the parent he wanted and needed—not only has the knowledge and ability to guide and support him, but will use both in his best interest, is what empowers the therapist's interventions, if they are reasonably accurate, to bring about fundamental changes in the way the patient deals with himself and the world. It is not uncommon to have a patient proudly tell some friend or family member what wonderful insights into himself he received thanks to therapy, how he can see the difference in his outlook and behavior, only to hear: "What are you paying that guy for? I've been telling you the same thing for years." The difference is that

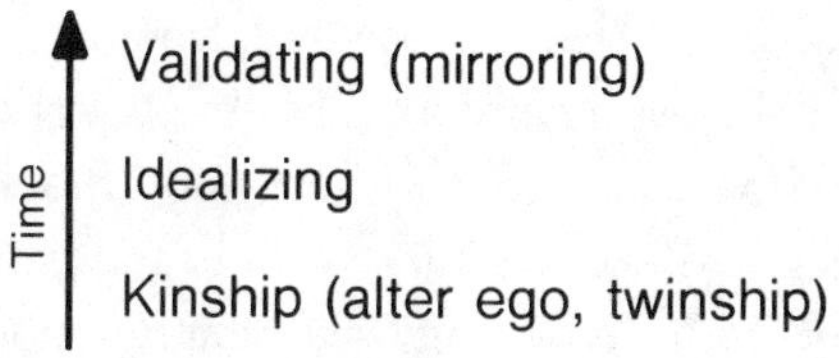

Validating (mirroring)

Idealizing

Kinship (alter ego, twinship)

FIGURE 2.1
Hierarchy of Selfobject Experiences

19

the spouse or friend was not vested, as the therapist is, with the trust that infants and children place in the idealized caregiving mother and father. During my student days, and many years before Kohut discovered and named this phenomenon, I experienced an unusually telling example of the idealizing transference and its effects.

## The Therapist as an Idealized Authority:
## Helen Pellman

The patient, Mrs. Helen Pellman, in her early thirties, was married and had raised several children. Her main complaint was that she felt frustrated, despairing, and angry. She had noted that in recent months she was becoming increasingly irritable, was sleeping poorly, and was gaining unwanted weight from trying to soothe herself with sweets. She feared that if she did not do something, she might have a nervous breakdown, and so decided to come to our clinic for help.

The patient said that her life was a series of disappointments. An intelligent, ambitious child, she had to accommodate herself to a mother who was fearful, superstitious, and probably mildly mentally retarded, and to a brutal father, whose only conversation with her came from the back of his hand. She escaped home when she was barely sixteen, dropping out of high school to marry a pleasant but ineffectual young man who was content to work for the city in a menial job. She fled her drab world with frequent visits to the public library, where she read indiscriminately and voraciously, but with increasing comprehension. What she learned of the world through her reading made her evermore dissatisfied with her lot. Now that her children were older, she had the time and the desire to improve her life, but her parental family, her husband, and her neighbors in her working-class neighborhood would not listen to or try to understand her.

And it was as a listener that she used me from the beginning to the end of her therapy. She had finally found in the therapeutic situation an educated person whom she could respect and who would pay close attention to her. She did not need me to talk, and indeed, when I first made some attempts at "interpreting," she simply ignored me and went on with her stream of thought. Fortunately I had enough sense to respond to her need and let her use me as she saw fit.

I saw Mrs. Pellman once weekly, and after a few months she looked better and felt much improved. It was obvious that she benefited markedly from the opportunity to review her life and vent her feelings in the sessions. She said she felt understood; that is, I appreciated her sense of frustration and her need to express herself. This understanding promoted the kinship experience on which her idealization—her trust in me—could be built. It no longer bothered me to sit quietly and attentively, often saying no more in the session than "hello" and "good-bye." Her initial despair gave way to an increasingly thoughtful assessment of her situation; her mood improved. At this point Mrs. Pellman concluded that the relief obtained from talking was not enough and that she would have to do something about her situation if anything further was to change.

I certainly felt like agreeing with her and supporting her conclusion, but I did not say anything. I was still under the influence of a model that dictated that to agree with a patient or to compliment her would at best be intrusive, at worst would gratify repressed forbidden wishes. The job of the therapist, I was taught, was limited to telling people what was wrong with them. Luckily, Mrs. Pellman was not thrown off track by my lack of validation and proceeded to secure a job that enabled her to move her family to a better neighborhood. A year and a half after starting to see me, she passed a high-school equivalency examination. She soon found herself ready to begin work on her undergraduate degree and signed up for night classes at a junior college. She now felt well enough to think about terminating her therapy. After a few more sessions during which we discussed that move, I concurred with her decision, and shortly thereafter she thanked me for all I had done, and left.

Mrs. Pellman had quickly formed an idealizing selfobject transference to me, crediting me, by virtue of my education and professional status, with the skills and powers that she needed to rely upon. Very much as a child will explore a strange room if a trusted parent is present, Mrs. Pellman was able to use her considerable intelligence, her desire to learn, and her will to succeed to examine her past and present life and to formulate and implement viable solutions for her dilemma. In terms of the developmental spiral (figure 1.1), Mrs. Pellman accommodated herself to a difficult environment, though the lack of communication throughout her life had deprived her of the personal rewards and validation of her interests, which she needed. As a result she had a severe self-esteem problem. And though I could not formulate the experience in this fashion at the time, it was through her deficient sense of self-esteem that I entered the pathological spiral and reversed it. Since she idealized me, my willingness and ability to take her seriously (implicitly validating her and her assessment of her situation) went a long way toward repairing her low opinion of herself. The decisions she then made and implemented continued to generate a sense of competence and self-esteem until she realized that she could, and wanted to, go forward by herself.

In retrospect, I would want to alter my therapeutic activity with Mrs. Pellman in two respects: First, I would not hesitate to validate explicitly both her evaluation of her situation and her efforts to improve it. Second, I would not "interpret," as I briefly tried to do, her need for achievement in terms of psychosexual issues and oedipal problems. At the time I was trained (and it is still not laid to rest in many quarters), dynamic or psychoanalytically oriented psychotherapy followed Freud's (1924) belief that psychological development and the vicissitudes of infantile sexuality were one and the same. I therefore briefly attempted to make connections for Mrs. Pellman between her wish to make the most of her potential as well as her frustration at not being able to do so, and her desire for an oedipal victory. This I would not attempt today, and fortunately, as I mentioned, she ignored my efforts in that direction. We know a great deal more about development now than we did in Freud's day. With a patient like Mrs. Pellman, oedipal interpretations do not address the central issues of her problem. Psychosexuality represents only one sector of the totality that is development. Other sectors, or aspects of development, that have been studied (figure 2.2) are cognition and affect, attachment, autonomy, and creativity. Others may well be added to that list in the future.

Upon reflection, I can see that Mrs. Pellman was in most respects a highly competent person. In terms of the various sectors of development, in all but one she gave evidence of more-than-adequate functioning: In the area of attachment, her relationships with her children, with her husband, and with me were all perfectly appropriate. She had no sexual complaints. Her creativity was demonstrated in her efforts both to cope with her very difficult socioeconomic circumstances and to expand her horizons through reading at the public library. Cognitive/

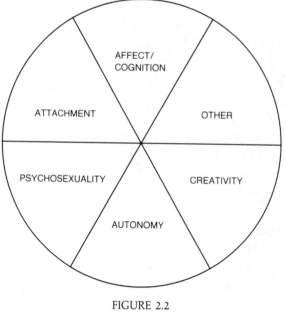

FIGURE 2.2
Sectors of Development

affective maturation was on a high level. In spite of her disappointments, her interest in life and her capacity to find pleasure in her relationships and activities had not flagged until some months prior to coming to see me. It was in the sector of autonomy that she had difficulty. Now that circumstances permitted, she could not separate herself sufficiently from her milieu to let her abilities carry her where they might. The incompetent aspect of her functioning affected her self-esteem, which in turn paralyzed her ability to make appropriate decisions. Her treatment reversed that situation and helped her to make the most of her potential in the sector of autonomy, as she had in other aspects of her development.

Development does not move in lock-step, and when first meeting a patient, a therapist must get an idea of the developmental sector involved in the patient's complaints. I think Miss Snow's principal defect, for example, was similar to Mrs. Pellman's in the sector of autonomy, that is, neither patient was able to act appropriately in her own interest; the admiral and would-be race car mechanic, I think now, suffered from problems in the creative sector. At least, that is how in retrospect I would have broached with him this difficult decision, and then seen what happened. Of course, nothing is written in stone, and one's initial impression can be changed whenever there is reason to do so. Furthermore, in any treatment in depth, one usually ends up dealing with various aspects of development in one form or another. It is nevertheless worthwhile to think of the developmental sector affected in a given patient when formulating a treatment plan. One's questions and interventions will then be guided by that determination and give a direction and a purpose to the therapeutic investigation that many patients need.

What happened with Mrs. Pellman was instructive but highly unusual. As a matter of fact, I have never had another case in which a patient talked herself well, needing only to experience the support of my attentive presence. Because of either a lack of clarity in my thinking, a failure to be empathic, or a patient's expected transference distortion and/or defense against insight (Basch 1988), there are times when the idealization wanes and is temporarily superseded by the patient's disappointment, anger, and frustration with the therapist and with the therapy. This situation must be dealt with actively by the therapist's interpretation of what the mood changes represent in terms of the present treatment relationship and/or how they repeat the patient's past experience. And when the idealizing transference is strong and steady, and under its aegis the patient is moving forward in activities and relationships, it is helpful for the therapist both to explain to the patient what is happening to advance maturation and improvement, and to validate the patient in what is happening. Examples of this will be given in cases to follow. First I wish to illustrate, however, what happens when anxiety interferes with the formation of an idealizing transference or when, having been present, the idealizing transference has essentially been lost.

## Resistance to Idealization: Vincent Vinci

A patient's inability to experience and/or the therapist's inability to mobilize an idealization—a situation usually due to a patient's intractable fears of that relationship—precludes a satisfactory therapeutic result. The patient who illustrates this dilemma, Mr. Vincent Vinci, was in psychoanalysis with me for four years. Mr. Vinci was a successful journalist, whose chief complaint was ostensibly in the developmental sector of creativity. Even though he was performing very well on his job, Mr. Vinci complained that he was unable to complete the novel he had been trying to write.

The patient had immersed himself in the work of Freud and Kohut for several years and understood a great deal about psychotherapy. He was very pleased that I respected his knowledge, treated him in collegial fashion, and did not look down on his amateur status. In letting me know that he was psychotherapeutically sophisticated, he was, it seems to me, stressing his need for kinship with me.

Although he had come to talk about problems in the developmental sector of creativity, at first he was focused on the sector of attachment. Mr. Vinci, an only child, had been raised by his mother. During the patient's early years, his father was away in military service. When his father returned from overseas, his mother went alone to meet the ship carrying the troops home. According to her, a quarrel ensued that alienated the two of them, and his father never came home. Subsequently, the patient had an ambivalent relationship with his mother. On the one hand, he recognized her devotion to him and, in turn, felt great responsibility for her. Yet he resented her possessive attitude and her attempt to direct his life. As an adult, he married over her objections and carried on a battle with his mother regarding her competitiveness with his wife and her attempt to usurp the upbringing of their two children.

We proceeded to work intensively in the sector of attachment and his relationship to his mother; it took, however, an unusual form. In discussing certain issues in the quarrelsome relationship with his mother, we reconstructed the repetitive patterns being played out and together thought about the early developmental as well as the immediate implications of what was happening. Mr. Vinci would come back in the next session and report that since seeing me he had, as he emphasized, *independently* attained new insight. He then repeated, almost word for word, the conversation he and I had had in the previous session. On one or two occasions, when I gently tried to point out to him that the two of us had come to these conclusions, he gave no indication that he had heard me. In other words, he behaved as if he could not afford to become conscious of the support I gave him and the insight I helped him achieve.

After several years, Mr. Vinci had greatly improved his relationship with his mother. He was able to be firm in defending his wife against the older woman's slurs and intrusions, and in protecting their right to rear their children as they saw fit. But as he noted ruefully, his creativity had not progressed. Periodically he was filled with grand plans for writing this, that, or the other aspect of his novel, or doing research to supplement the historical background of his tale, but all these plans came to naught. About this time a telling incident took place. The science editor of the newspaper for which he worked was ill, and the patient was assigned to take his place. One of the occasions he covered involved a medical meeting in which I happened to play a prominent part. Indeed, we saw each other there and exchanged greetings. In the following session, he spoke about the conference as if I had not been there, telling me who the various speakers were, what they had said, what had impressed him, and so on. He made no mention of my participation. When I reminded him that I had been on the podium and had spoken, he acknowledged that indeed he knew that was so. He totally dismissed the idea, however, that my presence at the meeting had any meaning for him, and he could not explain why he had felt it necessary to describe the details of the meeting to me. (This reaction is similar to what the psychiatrist Robert Jay Lifton [1986] has called *doubling*, a defensive compartmentalization of reality in the interest of avoiding shame and/or guilt.)

In subsequent sessions, his associations turned more and more to the father missing from his life. But though there was an intellectual insight into what his father's absence meant to him, he could not deal with it in the meaningful, that is, affective manner in which he had dealt with the historical relationship with his mother. It became increasingly clear that he was unable to form an idealizing relationship to me—to transfer to me a boy's concept of his father as powerful and stronger than he, a figure to be admired, envied, and challenged. This inability to overcome the defense against his need for the father precluded his working through the significance of the absent parent with me in therapy.

My own thoughts on the matter were twofold: On the level of psychosexuality, never having had a father to interact with, so that reality might have mitigated the fantasied punishment for competing with and challenging the powerful parent, he anticipated his father's enormous rage for taking possession of his mother and could not risk opening the competitive aspect of his character formation to therapeutic scrutiny. On another, earlier level in the sector of attachment, and perhaps even more significant, I thought Mr. Vinci's longing for a father

26

to trust and rely upon was so strong that to acknowledge it would have been experienced as too disorganizing. As Kohut (1971) has described, the unconscious urge to merge with the needed and admired other threatens the patient with a loss of self-cohesion. The fear is that to admit to such longing is an irrevocable step from which the self will never emerge as a functioning whole. It is the fear of no longer being in control of organizing one's experience that, as I have dealt with at length elsewhere (Basch 1988), generates anxiety, which leads to the formation of defense. In Mr. Vinci's case, the defense was probably what Freud (1915) called secondary repression, the ban on recalling the oedipal wishes, the fear of punishment, and the homophilic longing for the absent father. In the interest of maintaining the basic defense, Mr. Vinci mobilized mechanisms eliminating threatening perceptions (Basch 1974) and/or disavowed the affect that would have made those perceptions personally meaningful for him (Basch 1981; Jaffe 1988).

Although the symptoms had manifested themselves in the creative sector of development, the conflict responsible for his failure to function lay in both the sectors of psychosexuality and attachment. Unfortunately, my attempts to lead him to affectively meaningful insight came to naught. He had, after all, won the oedipal victory: Father was out of the picture and Mother preferred him. In Mr. Vinci's case, this resulted in an impenetrable sense of self-confidence, so that he never suffered the self-doubt and the shame in therapy that, when present, provide an entrée to the patient's problem areas.

In any case, some months after our encounter at the conference, the patient said that he had to terminate the therapy because of job-related impediments that precluded his continuing. He expressed gratitude for all we *had* accomplished and was quite aware that some things still needed to be done—perhaps at a later date when circumstances were more auspicious. Although his explanation sounded reasonable, it was clear to me that the logistics could have been dealt with had the patient not had to remove himself from therapy for unconscious reasons. My interpretations to that effect, however, fell on deaf ears and he left the analysis shortly thereafter.

In summary, when a patient has the capacity to idealize the therapist as once the powerful parents had been idealized in infancy and childhood, that attitude operates silently in the background, functioning as a base on which therapist and patient can stand as they uncover and resolve problems in the patient's development. When there have been problems with idealization in infancy and childhood, the patient's need for such an ideal can usually be met by the therapist in the evolution of the therapeutic process. When, however, the defense against coming to grips with idealizing needs is very strong, then that barrier of course becomes an issue for therapy. Often it can be resolved through clarification and interpretation; sometimes, as in the case of Mr. Vinci, one fails, and what needs to be done in therapy remains to a significant extent incomplete and unresolved.

Some years after Mr. Vinci had left analysis, he called me for an appointment. I learned when I saw him that a psychiatrist friend to whom he had voiced his disappointment at the incompleteness of our work, had told him that he should reenter analysis with an analyst deemed a more orthodox Freudian than myself. Mr. Vinci had followed the recommendation, but said that almost from the beginning of his two-year-long analysis, the analyst and he had been arguing about Mr. Vinci's "aggressive refusal to subordinate himself to the father/analyst's authority." Mr. Vinci asked me what I thought he should do. I said that under the circumstances it would be inappropriate for me to serve as his consultant and that he would have to discuss his wish for such consultation with his present analyst. To myself I noted that, once again, Mr. Vinci's inability to idealize the analyst precluded the formation of an oedipal transference and the recovery of repressed memories that probably related to his need for, and fear of, his father.

# CHAPTER 3

## Choosing a Therapeutic Approach

WITHIN A PERIOD OF A FEW MONTHS, I consulted with three women whose respective ages, backgrounds, and complaints were very much alike. All were in their middle thirties, all had lost or suffered the absence of at least one parent in childhood, and all came for consultation complaining primarily of disappointments in relationships with men. Based on what I heard from each of these would-be patients regarding their respective incompetencies and the sector of development affected, as well as their assets that had the potential for strengthening their self-esteem, I made tentative decisions regarding the approach to treatment calculated to help each of them. It turned out that, in spite of the superficial similarity of background and presenting complaint, each required a significantly different therapeutic approach. The application of the developmental model provided the rationale governing the technique used in their respective treatments.

### Focusing the Patient: Ms. Aye

The first patient, Ms. Aye, looked much younger than her thirty-four years, and her demeanor was similar to that of a frightened child. Both her parents had been anxious and overprotective, and Ms. Aye led a sheltered existence filled with prohibitions against what would be considered normal childhood activities. She was a day pupil at a parochial boarding school when her parents were killed in an automobile accident. Ms. Aye, then age sixteen, had no close relatives who would assume her care; she took up residence in the dormitory of her school and, upon graduation, became a novice in the religious order that was instructing her. Under these auspices she went to college and became a teacher, but it eventually became clear to her and to her superiors that she would not take the final vows binding her to the religious life. She made plans to leave the convent and, with the help of the sisters there, obtained a teaching job in Chicago.

She liked her work and was successful with the second-grade pupils in her charge. When not professionally occupied, however, she found herself lonely, frightened, and confused. She knew no one in Chicago, and she was too shy to make overtures for friendship to her fellow teachers. Her anonymity in a large city was accentuated because she had never lived in a situation that had not been mapped out for her. She was therefore pleased and relieved when a young man whom she met at a church social showed an interest in her and, in many ways, took over where her parents and the hierarchy of the convent had left off. She envisioned marriage and a family life, but a conflict developed and she found herself in a quandary.

Quite unsophisticated, she had only a vague notion that a psychotherapist might be able to help her. She wanted assistance in making a decision regarding her boyfriend, who was importuning her to have sexual intercourse with him while leaving the question of marriage indefinite. Afraid of losing the only person who she felt was interested in her and on whose guidance she had come to rely, and yet not wishing to engage in sexual intercourse without at least a promise of marriage, she became panicky and developed several somatic symptoms, which she herself attributed to "nerves." This diagnosis was corroborated by the school's physician, whom she consulted.

Although Ms. Aye's ostensible problem lay in the psychosexual sector of development—should she or should she not have a sexual relationship with her boyfriend—I thought that the issues immediately troubling her, that is, the focus of her incompetence, were in the sector of autonomy. Neither her life in her parental home nor her novitiate had given her the sense of self-reliance that one needs to live successfully alone or with another. As far as kinship and idealization went, I saw no problem in her ability to relate to me. Although she had never talked to a psychiatrist, she very soon became comfortable in the interview, demonstrating a range of appropriate affect and giving every indication that she trusted me to help her. Once I had provisionally evaluated Ms. Aye's situation, where and how should I intervene in the progression of the developmental spiral? Since she had posed the problem in terms of making a decision about her sexual life, I began there, anticipating that what I considered her real difficulty would come into focus.

Ms. AYE: My problem . . . is this the sort of thing you do?

THERAPIST: Help people examine and think about life's decisions? Yes.

Ms. AYE: Do you think you can help me?

THERAPIST: Yes.

Ms. AYE: What should I do?

THERAPIST: Well, why not look at what you've put on the table: most likely you have these headaches and stomachaches because of the pressure your boyfriend is putting on you. Do you feel any urge to have sex with him as things stand now?

Ms. AYE: Yes I do. I love Bill and I'm no prude. Even though I've never done that with anyone, we've experimented some and it feels good. And there was a boy before Bill that I liked—that's how I knew I couldn't be a nun—and I was plenty excited . . . *(patient pauses).*

THERAPIST: But?

Ms. AYE: I know what's going on out there. I don't need Bill to tell me that things aren't like they were twenty years ago. But he knows it's a mortal sin and so do I. I've waited this long, and I'll wait forever if that's the way it's going to be. Do you think that's neurotic, like Bill does?

THERAPIST: Quite the contrary. It certainly sounds as if you've thought this through and have come to a principled decision. It seems to me that if you were to go counter to your beliefs it would be a very unhealthy, to say nothing of an unhappy, introduction to what should be a very fulfilling part of life.

Although the patient here opened up the possibility of exploring her sexual life and past sexual experiences, I chose not to pursue these issues with her, though I anticipated that details of her history in all developmental sectors would emerge as therapy progressed. What would be gained for therapy at this point by hearing that she kissed this one and petted to orgasm with that one? She says she is no prude and has physical longings for Bill. Until proven otherwise, that tells me that her moral scruples are probably not just a red herring concealing an aversion to genital intercourse. More than that I don't feel I need to know about her sexual life at this point. What is important is that the decision concerning her sexual life leads to behavior that maintains her self-esteem.

In these opening interchanges of our work, Ms. Aye implicitly accepts me as an arbiter whose opinion carries the weight of authority, telling me that she looks to me to meet her need for an idealized other who can support and strengthen her self. This acceptance enables me to validate the patient in her behavior: Given her convictions regarding sexual behavior, I believe her decision is correct, and by letting her know that I am ready to see things through her eyes—to be empathic with her communication—I am strengthening the idealizing transference.

THERAPIST: *(Continuing)* But I don't think you need me to tell you your decision is the right one for you; you really knew that before you came here. The real issue is that you're frightened that Bill may lose interest in you and leave you as a result of your decision.

Ms. AYE: I don't know what I'd do without him. I was so lonely before . . .

THERAPIST: And scared.

Ms. AYE: Yes, I love Bill but I depend on him too. I mean, I didn't love him. . . . It wasn't love at first sight; that came later. At first it was such a relief not to be so alone. Before I met Bill, I just went to work and came home. I didn't read, I didn't even watch TV. I'd just sit and worry and go to bed and sleep as long as I could. Weekends were really bad. I'd go to church, but I don't think I heard a word.

THERAPIST: Sit and worry? What did you worry about?

Ms. AYE: I just felt lost. I just couldn't see living that way year after year, but I didn't know how I could change it.

THERAPIST: It was a big change in your life, being on your own . . .

Ms. AYE: All that changed when Bill came. Now I was doing things: I learned all there is in Chicago to do; I started finding my way around. I had someone to cook for once in a while. I mean I didn't even eat . . . ; it's no fun to cook just for yourself.

THERAPIST: Bill oriented and organized you to a way of life you'd never had, one in which the routines were not laid out as they are in college and in the convent.

Ms. AYE: That's right. Bill was a friend, I didn't think of him as a man at first, really. I think if I'd found a girlfriend it would have been the same thing.

THERAPIST: Exactly. I think that you're more scared right now of losing Bill, your friend and guide, than Bill, the man you love.

Ms. AYE: *(Starting to cry)* I just don't know what I'd do if it was like before. I guess I'm no better than my kids . . . I remember how scared I was the first day of kindergarten . . . I haven't changed . . .

THERAPIST: That's a good comparison. Like a child starting kindergarten, you're afraid that a new situation—a deviation from the familiar—is more than you can handle.

Ms. AYE: But what am I going to do without him? I haven't really talked to anyone else about what I'm feeling, or thinking, or doing.

THERAPIST: Number one, who says he's leaving? If he loves you, he might just stick around even though his needs and wishes don't control the situation. Number two, talking things over—that's what you came to me for. You're talking to me right now, and you're not alone. And why shouldn't we continue looking at your life together and seeing what you can do about your fears?

As you can see, in this first interview I strongly supported Ms. Aye's idea that she needed to see a therapist rather than commit herself to a liaison that went counter to her principles. Implicitly I made it clear that I was prepared to help her actively explore the reasons she lacked the confidence to manage her own life as well as to differentiate these issues from other decisions she had to make. In subsequent sessions, as her associations led her to the past, I entered the pathological spiral at the level of competence. I explained to her that what seemed to have happened was that her parents' overprotectiveness led her to believe she could not manage her own life in an age-appropriate way. She had become convinced that this was a very difficult task and was beyond her. She acknowledged that that was indeed the way she felt and behaved.

I suggested there was one important exception to that behavior: namely, she had told me that in the classroom she was very much in command of the situation and that her results with her pupils bore out her self-confidence as a teacher. Using this achievement as leverage, I led her to think about the world as a classroom in which all of us are children in various stages of maturity. As she herself had said, she looked at the world like a child starting kindergarten—things that later become ordinary seem at first overwhelming and terrifying.

I helped her to see that she already knew a great deal more than she realized by virtue of managing her apartment, paying her bills, cooking her meals, doing her laundry, and so on—competent behavior for which she gave herself no credit. At first she thought I was joking; these seemed such ordinary, even trivial accomplishments, but she soon realized that I was serious. By letting her know that I respected her capacity to function and that I did not consider her basically so different from everyone else, myself included, she experienced a kinship, where previously there had been only alienation. As she began to experiment on her own, with much less reliance on Bill's initiative, I underscored and gave her my approval for various tentative steps toward independence, and thus validated her behavior (see also Kramer 1989).

As she found herself functioning very differently in life, she recovered memories that led her to realize she had been angry for a long time at her parents. She now felt that her fears were to a great extent an accommodation to their needs. It was *they* who were afraid that if she became too independent some harm might befall her, and they could not take that risk—a risk that every parent owes a child. She saw that her parents had led her to believe that life was a great deal more complicated and dangerous than it really was. She mourned the time she had lost but vowed to make it up to herself.

After about a year of twice-weekly therapy, Ms. Aye was a very different person. Far less dependent on her boyfriend, she now successfully renegotiated their relationship, suggesting that they see each other less frequently and give themselves one year in which to decide whether they would be married or go their separate ways. And as the summer vacation was approaching, which coincided with the time we had planned for terminating her treatment, she planned a trip that would take her to countries she had always wanted to see but had never dared even to think of visiting alone.

I have outlined here how I came to the provisional conclusion that Ms. Aye's search for competence—her efforts to maintain a sense of a cohesive, functioning self—hit a snag in the developmental sector of autonomy. Her behavior toward me in the session and her statements about her relationship with others gave me reason to believe that she was transference-ready. She was prepared to fulfill her need for an idealizing and mirroring selfobject experience if I was able to respond appropriately to these needs. I chose to intervene first at the decision-making level of the developmental spiral in the psychosexual sector and then, when her fear of behaving autonomously emerged, I intervened at the level of competence. This brings us to an issue not yet discussed. Deciding where one should intervene still leaves open the question of *how* one should intervene: how can one reach this particular patient most effectively at this particular time?

There are many ways I could have attempted to get where I believed Ms. Aye needed to go. When Ms. Aye said, "My problem . . . is this the sort of thing you do?," I could have replied: "Well, why not let me hear more of your concerns about that?" When she asked whether I could help her, I could have been much less definite and left it open-ended. Instead, I made it clear that she was in the right place and that I thought I could help her. I then suggested a topic for exploration, putting Ms. Aye in the position of first having to look at her feelings around sexual behavior and then, though I did not force it, I took an active therapeutic stance in guiding her associations toward her difficulty with autonomy. I also had no hesitation in supporting her convictions, stilling her doubts, and strengthening her self-esteem in relation to her view of sexual morality. There were a great many things I could have done that I chose not to do.

In addition to not exploring her sexual history, I also did not focus on issues around her parents' death, life in the convent, and her decision to leave, and so on. As with most patients—especially cooperative, verbal patients—there are many interesting, worthwhile avenues to examine; yet, since we cannot be everywhere at the same time, we must make choices. One way to do that, familiar to most of us from our training, is to let the patient decide: "Why not go ahead and tell me whatever you're thinking about—just let your mind go where it will." Instead, I went to the other end of the spectrum and, at least at first, pretty much focused the session and guided the patient in her associations. Why one technique rather than another? How I choose to intervene in a particular case and/or at a particular time depends on the stage or level of the patient's pathology.

## The Evolution of the Sense of Self

The psychoanalyst and infant researcher Daniel Stern (1985) has established that there is a developmental line for the formation of the sense of self, very much as there is for cognition or for physical skills like walking (figure 3.1). Stern describes the following progression for self-development: emergent, core, subjective, verbal, and narrative sense of self. These subdivisions, respectively, embody the five basic tasks involved in what I call the search for competence: orientation, adaptation, affective validation, reflection, and evaluation (figure 3.2). Once we have determined the nature of a patient's "incompetence"—the patient's loss of control over his capacity to adapt to his circumstances while fulfilling reasonable personal goals—we apply our understanding of these steps

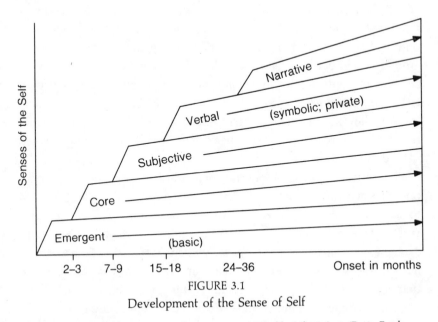

FIGURE 3.1
Development of the Sense of Self

Adapted from Daniel N. Stern, *The Interpersonal World of the Infant*. (Basic Books, 1985, p. 32). Reprinted by permission.

to assess the level of dysfunction and the most appropriate intervention to help the patient gain or regain a healthy self-esteem.

In the first two months after birth, the primary caregiver, usually the mother, orients her baby to the rhythm of events that make up his schedule—feeding, sleeping, playing, bathing—a pattern of expectation is set up that forms the basis for the sense of what Stern calls the *emergent self*.

In the third month of life the infant gives evidence that he now experiences himself as the invariant originator of different activities and the invariant receiver of shifting perceptions. This experience of being the fixed or centered locus in a constantly changing world gives rise to the sense of the *core self*. It is during this period that the infant actively participates in developing patterns or scripts for dealing with life's needs and vicissitudes: how to get one's thumb into one's mouth; what to do if a thumb is not available, and so on. It is during this period that the baby demonstrates effectance pleasure, or pleasure in being a cause (White 1959; Broucek 1979).

At about seven months of age, the *sense of a subjective self*, a sense of self in relation to another, is added to the sense of an emergent and core self. Now a baby's feeling of well-being depends not just on successful functioning but also on recruiting the feedback from his mother or another audience, signaling that that other person is participating vicariously in his experience. Stern calls this the infant's need for *affect attunement*.

The self is further enhanced by what Stern calls the *verbal sense of self*, the ability to use words and other symbols to create the private world of reflection. This stage marks the end of infancy and the beginning of

| Domain of Self-Development | Associated Life Task |
|---|---|
| 1. Emergent (basic) sense of self | Orientation |
| 2. Core sense of self | Adaptation |
| 3. Subjective sense of self | Affective Validation |
| 4. Verbal (symbolic, private) sense of self | Reflection |
| 5. Narrative sense of self | Evaluation |

FIGURE 3.2
The Search for Competence

childhood. Symbolizing, like the muscular coordination of the core self, adds to and further strengthens the sense of self. When symbolizing comes on line, it makes evocative memory and the objectification of experience possible; that is, unlike the infant who can only react, the child can now begin to use imagination to recall the past and plan for the future. Since not only words but other symbols, such as musical tones and pictorial images, permit us to reflect upon past experiences and create new ones, I think of this category as the *symbolic sense of self.* I also think of this category as the *private self,* because symbolizing activity forms a personal mental preserve that no one can share unless we permit it. Symbolic activity creates the two realities in which we live—the objective world of meaning that is consensually validatable and shared, and the coexisting subjective one in which meaning is arrived at idiosyncratically (Palombo 1991). It is in the latter that the newly found capacity for fantasy distorts experience and gives rise to what Freud (1915) called primary process thinking: unconscious hopes, wishes, and fears whose power to recruit affect exercises a strong, sometimes overpowering influence on the search for competence.

Finally, though he does not discuss it in his 1985 book, Stern (1989) tells us that at about three years of age, the *narrative sense of self* is ushered in: in my terms, the ability to describe one's decision-making process and its results to oneself or to another person, opening the way for evaluating one's ideas and plans through either objective reflection or through actively recruiting consensual validation.

As Stern makes clear, once in place, each of the described functions— becoming oriented, developing coping strategies, recruiting validating affective participation, engaging in symbolic objectification, and evaluating concepts and plans—coexist, continue to expand in depth and breadth, and support and maintain an ever-evolving and maturing sense of self. Whatever phenomenological label one assigns to it, a patient's problem from an operational perspective expresses a failure in the search for competence and a resulting impairment in self-esteem. The patient's level of functioning, therefore, as he presents himself to the therapist is at least a useful beginning in formulating one's technical approach. So when I say that the manner in which I intervene in a given case is determined by the patient's level of functioning in the area of his pathology, it is Stern's hierarchical description of the formation of the sense of self that I have in mind (figure 3.2): How well is the patient oriented to his situation? How appropriate are his strategies for coping with the problem? Does he feel all alone or not? Can he think clearly about his difficulties? Is he able to describe them to me? What I learn governs what I then do therapeutically. Take, for example, the patient who is well oriented, coping effectively, but feels alone, lost, and unhappy because of an inability to get emotional feedback. Such a situation calls for a technique different from one used with the patient who finds that he understands what is needed but cannot formulate appropriate strategies to meet the challenge facing him. This technique will differ from that used with the patient who seems to function on automatic pilot, going into action without being able to reflect on the possible consequences of his behavior, and so on.

To return now to Ms. Aye. As I heard Ms. Aye's story, I listened not only for its content but also for the highest level on which she was still functioning in the area of her difficulty, as both she and I saw it. Ms. Aye believed that what confronted her was a decision about her sexual behavior. It was evident that she did not lack clear guidelines or scripts for what was acceptable to her in that regard, and that she received ample affective support for her view from her co-religionists. She had certainly reflected on the validity of her belief and found it sound. Support for the narrative sense of self came not only from her religious ideals but from her boyfriend. Bill, too, shared her moral position and gave her consensual validation.

Bill was apparently willing to cast aside his scruples, however, and, ostensibly, what she needed from me in the sector of psychosexual development was an intervention on the level of the narrative self, validating her right to refuse Bill sexual intercourse outside of marriage. Or was she perhaps looking to me for permission to cast aside religious restrictions and give in to Bill's pressure? I believed that I had disproved the latter when I established that she was not using her ethical position to conceal an obvious sexual problem. Why then did she need a therapist to get consensual validation for a position already amply buttressed by her religious teaching and, as far as she was concerned, by God? My answer, as you know, was that she was not here for that. She had already made a decision not to engage in premarital sex, and the consequences of her decision were what she feared: she anticipated she would once again be left alone to face the world, and that terrified her. Now we were in the developmental sector of autonomy, and here was a very different story. Ms. Aye felt panicked when she tried to think of being without Bill to help her negotiate the world apart from her work and her housekeeping. She had not been able to trust herself to develop the scripts that might have given her confidence to adapt to unfamiliar situations and find friends and interests in a new environment.

Even more basic, the idea of having to find her way panicked her. She had no sense that now, with the experiences she had had under Bill's tutelage, she might well be able to get along independently. Like a newborn infant, Ms. Aye needed the orienting selfobject experience that a mother gives her baby as she acquaints it with its new existence. That line of reasoning led me to decide that rather than leaving her on her own in the therapy, I would make it clear to Ms. Aye that she and I would look together at the world she feared. Of course, Ms. Aye was not an infant. In many respects she had attained a highly functional sense of self. As I described, I used what had gone right with her to help her gradually correct what had gone wrong in her development. Her readiness to accept my offer of kinship and her idealization—the hope that I could and would help her—made my efforts effective and let her benefit from the validation or mirroring that I gave her as she let herself move forward. Once she was able to think for and about herself, she no longer needed as much of my guidance. We worked then on the level of the subjective self, where my therapeutic activity consisted mainly of validating and appreciating her new-found capacities.

Her strengthened self now permitted Ms. Aye to undo aspects of her defensive repression of memories and gain insight into the formation of her character structure. She could recall and reexamine those episodes of childhood that let us understand how her parents' fears had forced her into a risk-aversive timidity that served to avoid precipitating *their* anxiety—a position she could now discard.


## Behind Anxiety: Ms. Bee

Ms. Bee called me on the recommendation of a friend acquainted with my work. She said she wanted to discuss some personal problems. She was thirty-three years old and had already been divorced twice, and now found herself once again in a difficult relationship with a man.

Although she sounded friendly on the phone, during our first session she was angry and demanding with me. She found fault with me and with my office, and announced that, in general, she felt psychiatry was a hoax. In other words, she repudiated the offer of kinship implied by our meeting. Her behavior seemed to demonstrate a lack of competence in the sector of attachment. If this attitude was typical of her, or of her way of dealing with interpersonal situations, she would most likely structure things in a way that would distance people from her. Since I was curious about that, and she seemed to be getting no further than telling me how I was wasting my life as a psychiatrist, I decided to enter the pathological spiral by calling attention to her behavior to see whether this trend could be reversed. Accordingly, I asked her what she hoped to accomplish in consulting with me, and how she saw her diatribe as getting the job done. Ms. Bee was surprised and visibly hurt; she had heard herself say that she was fearful that perhaps no one could help her. She added that she had had several disappointing attempts at therapy over the years.

THERAPIST: Well, that's a whole different story, isn't it? I'm glad I asked. It's a good thing that we are in a psychotherapeutic situation where your communications are examined rather than taken at face value. Under other circumstances, I would just have withdrawn from you and gone off into a corner to lick my wounds; I would never have known the nature of the fears behind your anger.

Ms. BEE: *(In a very different voice and with a much changed attitude)* That's just what always happens to me . . .

THERAPIST: Yes, go on.

Ms. BEE: *(Shamefacedly)* My last boyfriend called me a "castrating bitch" when he left.

THERAPIST: Did you have any idea why he said that?

Ms. BEE: No, I just thought it was his problem.

THERAPIST: In all probability he did contribute his share to the breakup, but, based on what we've been through just now, a failure to communicate what you really meant undoubtedly also played a part.

During this dialogue, Ms. Bee's voice lost its stridency and became soft and appealing. This change indicated to me that I had reached her on the level of kinship, and, as shown by her tone of voice and her cooperation with the interview, that she now looked to me for help: she was beginning to extend tendrils of what eventually could become idealization—a beginning hope in my ability to help her. This impression was further strengthened by the fact that she now went on spontaneously to volunteer her personal history.

Ms. Bee had been raised in a family in which the mother was the primary breadwinner; the father, a failed writer, was the parent who was in the home most of the time and took care of the patient, an only child. When Ms. Bee was eleven years old, her father, without any warning, committed suicide. As if that were not sufficiently traumatic, her mother did not help the child with the loss. Far from grief-stricken, she soon married the paramour who had been waiting in the wings.

In her adult life, it seemed to me, Ms. Bee reenacted with the various men in her life both the longing to be cared for, as she had been by her father, and the conviction that all men were fatally flawed and would disappoint her. As she talked more about her relationships with various men, I heard a repetitive pattern of impatience: the need to come to premature closure—to bind herself quickly to a likely man only to be disappointed and angry when he turned out to be wanting in one or another respect. She would latch on to a man who had expressed interest in her and behave as if her psychological need for a relationship was also his. She was quick to have sex, seeing it as a forerunner of the deeper intimacy she craved. Often, however, the man's attraction was more physical than emotional. Then the signs that he did not share her sense of permanence and intimacy would provoke Ms. Bee to lash out viciously in her disappointment. It would not be long before the man would distance himself from her and her "castrating" behavior.

Based on what I had heard, and given that the patient was now ready to hear me and to participate, I formulated an approach to therapy. Ms. Bee's immediate difficulty seemed located in the core-self aspect of the attachment sector, as suggested by the self-defeating programs or scripts she had developed for forming relationships with men. I chose to intervene actively in examining these with her, beginning at the behavioral level of the pathological spiral. When she brought it up in our second session, therefore, I suggested to Ms. Bee that we look together at her recently terminated attempt at a relationship with Ted, who also happened to be her employer. Based on her previous experiences in therapy, Ms. Bee was quick to make connections between her longing for her boss, a man some seventeen years older than she, and her need for the father who had left her so suddenly and in such a terrible way. Some of her initial contempt crept back into her voice as she questioned my refusal to be satisfied with her conclusions and insisting instead that she describe in detail both the man involved and the manner of their interaction. In discussing the occasion of their last quarrel, she mentioned that it had taken place in a restaurant. "Which one?" I wanted to know. When it turned out to be a very posh place, I asked, "How come? Did you always go to such expensive places when you went out?"

In spite of her disdain for my interest in details, as opposed to doing "real therapy" in which the "why" rather than the "what" was the focus, she did go along with me and let me draw the story of that one incident out of her.

I had no worry that she would not do so. Unless the longing for an idealizing selfobject experience is too anxiety provoking, the patient's need for the therapist's support, interest, and positive regard is such that the patient will veer in the direction that the therapist explicitly or implicitly indicates he wishes the patient to take. This does not mean, however, that the patient will get better at the suggestion of, and to "please," the therapist—the so-called transference cure. On the contrary, a stalemate in therapy will often result—and may last for years until patient and therapist part out of exhaustion—if the therapist does not address the patient's developmental needs in at least a peripherally appropriate manner. The patient stays in treatment because the therapist potentially embodies a needed selfobject experience, but that potential must be made actual through interventions that address the specific issues with which the patient is struggling. The patient's compliance and cooperation are, therefore, in themselves not an indicator that all is well; rather, they signal that an idealizing need is being met. The signs of progress that the therapist looks for are alterations in the patient's decision making and/or behavior, competence, and self-esteem. These are the indicators that things are moving in the right direction.

As the case of Mrs. Pellman (pp. 20–23) demonstrates, occasionally there are patients who need only the opportunity for idealization to make progress, and in every therapy there are times when, supported by kinship and idealization, the patient moves forward despite the therapist's misunderstanding of what is going on. In the main, however, it is the therapist's job to move the therapy along based on an understanding of the patient's central developmental issues.

As Ms. Bee reconstructed the details of her last date with Ted, I learned that he had chosen to go to an elegant restaurant to celebrate his fiftieth birthday. The occasion was marred for him because neither of his adolescent children—both of whom were living with his former wife—had called to congratulate him. Ms. Bee said this "freaked her out"—one of many expressions that I was to hear that addressed affective issues but were too indefinite to let me or, more importantly, her, understand what she was actually experiencing. As I focused on this interaction between her and Ted, I learned that any dysphoria Ms. Bee experienced evoked anger in the form of an attack on the self-esteem of whoever had made her anxious. Once I had put this scenario together, I explained to the patient what I thought was happening to her, very much as I am doing here. I dealt with her reaction and dissected the stages of the script she had written for occasions similar to the one with Ted. Most important, I stressed that her anger was a reaction to anxiety, which is a general reaction to an inability to create order in one's world—in other words, to maintain a reasonable degree of competence (Basch 1988).

The question then became, I said to Ms. Bee, what had Ted's complaint about his children and his ex-wife's conduct elicited in her? In short, she experienced that another's emotional preoccupation deprived her of what she needed and, despite the counterproductive consequences of her behavior, led her to attack the person whose attention and concern she was so afraid of losing. It was not until several months later that she recalled incidents that let me interpret to Ms. Bee that this behavior was her only way of occasionally getting her mother to focus on her instead of on herself—a crucial insight that let Ms. Bee understand that it was the man's *mothering* that she both desperately sought and consistently undermined.

But long before that point in the therapy, I continued to work with Ms. Bee around the issue of understanding and articulating her affective reactions. We unpacked not only "freaked out" but also such expressions as "super," "zonked," "off-the-wall," "stressed out," and the ubiquitous, "well, you know."

Ms. Bee's maturational arrest in the developmental sector of attachment had not given her the opportunity to grow in the affective aspect of the cognitive/affective sector. We reversed this process. As Ms. Bee learned through my repeated interventions to understand and express herself affectively, over several months her capacity for relating appropriately to others greatly improved. Gradually the therapeutic process came to be governed by her agenda. At times she would recount episodes in her present life, at other times, events from her past. Usually one or the other of us would then make the connection between the past and the present. In therapy I was now able to range over all the aspects of the sense of self—sometimes orienting her to a situation, other times offering consensual validation for reflections she presented for consideration, now examining her way of coping, and perhaps later in the same session validating through affect attunement some other experience. Similarly, the focus of my efforts in the developmental spiral depended on where her thoughts led. On the whole, once she was able to respond in an affectively appropriate manner to the vicissitudes of her life, we focused much less on behavior as such and much more on the implicit decision-making process behind her actions as well as the effect of her new-found competence on her self-esteem.

## A Psychoneurotic Patient: Ms. See

Ms. See, a thirty-six-year-old, single, accomplished advertising executive, related to me in a warm and straightforward manner. She said that she had a great desire to be married and have a family and was worried that her child-bearing years would end before she had a chance for motherhood. There had been no lack of suitable men in her life, but it seemed that no matter how promising her initial relationship with a man, none of these auspicious beginnings ever came to fruition. She was aware that with each of these men she repeated a cycle of self-defeating interaction that she could recognize but not control.

She had been raised in a well-to-do Jewish family. Her much-loved father died of heart disease when Ms. See was twelve years old. She described how she, her two younger brothers, and her mother had clung to and supported each other during this difficult time and how her extended family had rallied around them. She felt, once she recovered from her grief, that her adolescence had been a satisfying and rewarding one. When the patient was eighteen and about to leave home for college, her mother married a man whose appearance and character, the patient said, were very much like her father's.

As I listened to Ms. See describe her life, I heard a great deal that was on the side of competence. She talked about her work enthusiastically: she enjoyed the advertising business and the challenge of designing the approach that met a client's needs. What she said and, what is usually more important, the feelings she communicated when she spoke, told me that the developmental sectors of autonomy and creativity were in good order. She had a rich social life with good friends of both sexes and got along well with her mother and stepfather. I concluded, therefore, that the sector of attachment did not present major difficulties. It was only when she spoke of what she called her most recent failure with a man with whom she had been involved romantically for some time, that her affective tone changed from lively and communicative to puzzled, tense, and distressed. She could not understand her inability to respond physically during sexual intercourse though she was orgasmic in solitary masturbation. She regarded herself a failure, less than a woman. In this area her otherwise healthy self-esteem had suffered. The dysphoria and self-doubt aroused by what she felt was her sexual failure eventually made her "depressed" and led to the breakup of all her romantic relationships.

Ms. See's complaint pointed to the psychosexual sector of development as the most likely source of her difficulty. I looked for immediate causes that might account for her incompetence and the resultant loss of self-esteem, but I could find none. She was not hampered consciously by any inhibition around sexual relations, enjoyed her partners' sexual attention, and only became close with men whom she liked and who seemed to care for her—in other words, her decision making seemed soundly based, as did her behavior. I concluded that, in all probability, her sexual problem was evidence of a psychoneurosis: that is, her symptom was, as Freud (Breuer and Freud 1893–1895; Freud 1926) originally described it, an expression of a conflict around early childhood sexuality, which was buried like a foreign body in an otherwise healthy character. As with Ms. See, in these patients one encounters a mature self that offers no obvious handhold for immediate therapeutic interventions. In such a situation, a highly specialized form of psychotherapy, psychoanalysis, is needed. I have elsewhere given a clinical example illustrating the course of psychoanalytic treatment in the psychoneurotic

46

patient (the case of "Mr. Neubach," Basch 1988). Here I want to call attention only to the contrast between this form of treatment and psychotherapeutic technique that does not have a psychoanalytic goal.

## Insight Therapy: Regressive and Progressive

Psychoanalysis is a technique that reverses the developmental process. Patients such as Miss Snow, Roberta, Ms. Aye, and Ms. Bee come to us with symptoms indicative of an impaired sense of self. The defect in the sense of self, or the attempted compensation for it—like Ms. Bee's anger, for example—is usually apparent in the patient's way of relating to the therapist. Guided by the developmental model, the therapist can formulate a treatment plan utilizing the therapeutic relationship to highlight the difficulties and to intervene in ways that will foster maturation and repair the damage to the patient's sense of self—a progressive approach. Psychoanalysis, by contrast, uses a regressive technique.

Neurotic patients like Ms. See relate to us and to others in mature, reasonable ways—their suffering is private and the symptoms seemingly make no sense. As does the surgeon, in a favorite analogy of Freud's, the analyst must first cut through the normal layers of character formation to expose what lies beneath the surface. Using the developing sense of self described earlier to explain Freud's method, I conceptualize the process as follows. The patient lies on the couch; the analyst's chair is out of sight behind him. This arrangement deprives the patient of many of the clues we all use from infancy on to orient ourselves to others and maintain the basic, emergent sense of self. The patient's supine position emphasizes that no activity other than speech is acceptable in the analysis. All of the patient's scripts that depend on studying another's facial expressions and bodily movements to get guideposts for maintaining social situations and strengthening the core self are useless to him here.

Furthermore, the analyst's emotional reactions to what the neurotic patient says are not verbally expressed. The analyst listens and expresses neither approval nor disapproval. This affective neutrality severely limits the functioning of the patient's subjective sense of self, which is ordinarily guided by the emotional feedback given directly and indirectly by those around us. In the analysis of a neurotic patient, the analyst usually does not answer questions and refrains from commenting on the ideas the patient expresses, depriving the patient of the opportunity for consensual validation—the input potentiated by the narrative sense of self. The technique used in the analysis of psychoneurotic patients, therefore, operates to focus the patient on the symbolic (verbal) or private self during the psychoanalytic session, and it is here that the patient's pathology, which is generating the patient's dysfunction and symptoms, is located. This calculated stimulus deprivation creates an artificial regression and promotes the anxiety that comes with loss of control (incompetence) over the self system.

The reàson that an artificial therapeutic anxiety must be produced is that as the patient attempts to cope with this anxiety to restore his sense of self, he gradually mobilizes the hidden, but affectively overladen hopes, wishes, and fears of his private self and transfers them to the analyst. It is the transference repetition and the emotion-laden new edition of old traumatic experiences that gives the analyst the opportunity to help the patient obtain insight into the causes of his illness, and, through that understanding, to foster the resumption of the developmental processes impaired by the earlier trauma.

I hope this description of psychoanalytic technique, in contrast to psychotherapy generally, will clarify and eliminate some misconceptions harmful to our practice. Psychoanalysis is a therapy that is based on therapeutic regression; most of our patients, however, are already regressed (immature in significant respects) and are, at best, not helped, and at worst, harmed by the therapist's withdrawal. For example, Roberta, the abused three-and-a-half-year-old patient, would have only further drawn into her shell if the therapist had not been actively forthcoming and helped the child to repair the damage done to her self system. Working with a patient with an anxiety neurosis whose symptom takes the form of a fear of sudden death, one may just quietly sit there, unmoved by the panic in his voice, and say calmly, "Tell me what else occurs to you," but would one want to say that to Miss Snow? No. Whereas in the analysis of a psychoneurotic patient, an artificial transference neurosis must first be fostered so as to use the attendant anxiety to promote the patient's development, this technique is not called for in most cases where the regression and the accompanying anxiety are already all too evident.

Psychoanalysis is often mistakenly equated with insight therapy or, another way of putting it, with making the unconscious conscious. Yet in their respective psychotherapies, Ms. Aye became conscious of the anger at her parents for infantilizing her, while Ms. Bee gained insight into her previously unconscious need for a mother she never had. And so it is with most patients who cooperate with the psychotherapeutic process and eventually work with the therapist on the level of the symbolic or private self—reflecting about their reflections, so to speak. In these patients, too, what has been unconscious becomes conscious and expands the patient's insight into his or her manner of functioning.

Psychoanalysis is one way of promoting insight into the operation of the self system, but it is not the only way. Extrapolating to other patients with other pathologies the artificial deprivation of the analyst's input, which is necessary in the treatment of psychoneurotic patients, has created tremendous harm (see, for example, Firestein 1978; Malcolm 1980; Schlessinger and Robbins 1983). Indeed, as Kohut (1971) demonstrated, the psychoanalytic treatment of patients with narcissistic personality disorders does not benefit from the so-called classic or traditional posture that is appropriately used with psychoneurotic patients. Among many patients repression is not the main defense against anxiety-provoking experiences (Basch 1985), yet the extent of their pathology is such that they too would benefit from an analytic approach, that is, emphasizing the formation of, and insight into, the transference, rather than—as in psychotherapy—using the transference to bring about insight into, and resolution of, particular problem areas. Both psychoanalysis and psychotherapy, when successful, enhance and promote the patient's development: Psychoanalysis works from the bottom up, exploring the origin of the patient's character formation so as to promote insight into his or her present situation; insight or dynamic psychotherapy works from the top down—that is, it examines the patient's present situation in order to understand how he or she functions now, thereby promoting in the patient insight into the vicissitudes that have formed his or her character.

Analysts and psychotherapists trained to look upon the traditional analytic model as the paradigm for good therapy have, with the best of intentions, made stimulus deprivation a therapeutic virtue and, like the still occasionally useful medical practice of bleeding, have applied it with a universality that has done more harm than good. Using Kohut's developmentally appropriate extension of the transference concept, I have already suggested how patients with other than psychoneurotic problems might be treated. This brings up an interesting issue. The opening phases of therapy with such patients would be the same whether I planned to use psychoanalysis or psychotherapy. Indeed, when the defense is not repression of memory but, as it is in most of our patients, either disavowal of affect, withdrawal from stimulation, or failure of symbolization (primary repression), then, thanks to Kohut, the division between psychoanalysis and psychotherapy becomes much less sharp. I have elsewhere (1988), in the "Esther Romberg" case, described a treatment in which my aim was a psychotherapeutic, problem-oriented one, but in which the patient spontaneously mobilized a regressive transference and, without the benefit of either couch or four-times weekly sessions, proceeded to an analytic result.

One can base one's decision about using analysis or dynamic psychotherapy on the patient's readiness or impediment to forming a selfobject transference. The more a patient's need for a selfobject response is itself fraught with anxiety, the more likely a psychoanalytic approach will be needed, for it is in the analytic regression that the patient's fears about the selfobject transference become clear and can be dealt with (see also figure 5.1 and the attendant discussion). When the developmental problem is out in the open, other psychotherapies can usually deal with it directly.

Another misconception that needs to be cleared up is the notion that psychoanalysis is per se a more complete form of treatment than is psychotherapy. As the case of Vincent Vinci illustrates, the sector of attachment and the pathology in the sense of the subjective self lent itself to analysis; the symbolic self and its psychosexual/oedipal issues did not. I believe that in terms of a patient's functioning and self-esteem, which are, after all, the pragmatic measures of the treatment's success, Ms. Aye's and Ms. Bee's respective psychotherapies were more effective than was Mr. Vinci's psychoanalysis. What is important for our patients is the therapist's optimal responsiveness (Bacal 1985), and what that may be is determined by each patient's developmental issues as they emerge at a particular time in the therapy (Holinger 1989).

# CHAPTER 4

## Dealing with Shame

$P$ROBABLY THE MOST COMMON PROBLEM that the psychotherapist must deal with in his patients is that of shame (Nathanson, in press). Shame is a particular form of distress generated by the inadequate reduction of tension associated with the loss of the other's ongoing or expected emotional participation, which Stern (1985) has called affect attunement. It is the isolation, the loss of intimacy with the other—shown literally in children when, in response to disapproval (parental disgust), the child's head droops and eye contact with the parent is broken—that is so painful and forms the basis for the sense of worthlessness that is the hallmark of the shame experience. Painful as it is, shame is basically a protective measure. It is a signal that whatever we are doing is not working and should be stopped (Basch 1988; Nathanson 1987). The outward manifestation of shame—the hang-dog appearance, with the face often suffused with blood—is also a signal to the other that help is needed in reestablishing positive communication. The response to that signal has a great deal to do with whether shame becomes a manageable experience or whether the fear of shame becomes, as in some extreme cases, the focus around which character development is organized.

In their effort to learn and adapt, infants and children, while also asserting their autonomy, often create situations that meet with disapproval. Optimally, the shame they then experience is quickly dissipated when they are forgiven, and a better way of dealing with whatever they were trying to do is taught to them. What is very damaging, however, is the situation in which the sense of shame attaches not to a particular mistake or deed but to one's self. The conviction that it is not what one has done but that one's own self is worthless is a devastating experience. People go to great lengths to avoid its repetition, often stifling initiative and undermining their potential for fear of failing and reawakening that devastating sense of total unacceptability.

As the following two clinical vignettes will illustrate, how a therapist understands shame and what significance he attaches to it is central for its successful clinical management.

## A Theory That Failed: Herbert Boltz

Early in my psychiatric training, I saw a Mr. Herbert Boltz, a reserved, noncommunicative, thirty-year-old, married salesman, who came to the clinic complaining that for no apparent reason he always felt moderately anxious and depressed. He was not given to introspection and clearly expected me to do or say something that would make him feel better.

His history gave me no immediate clues as to how I could help him. Our weekly sessions were taken up with matter-of-fact recitals of his daily activities and his complaining that he was not getting anywhere in his treatment. Feeling stymied, I waited and hoped that whatever unconscious fantasies were causing his distress would sooner or later lead him to say something that would provide an entrée to more meaningful work. After some months of this, he hesitantly said that there was something from his past that he had not revealed and could not tell me. Certain that this was the key I had been looking for, I spent the next few sessions urging him to overcome his reluctance and tell me what was troubling him.

Finally, during one of our appointments, he took a deep breath, screwed up his courage, and told me the awful secret he had been harboring: When he was a little boy attending kindergarten, he had lost bowel control and defecated in his pants. He paused, and I asked in a sympathetic voice what had happened then. Mr. Boltz just sat in his chair and hung his head. I saw that his face was flushed, and I think there may have been tears in his eyes.

I do not know what I had expected to hear, but this was certainly disappointing, or, perhaps more accurately, confusing. What was so earth-shaking about this incident, and why was it so difficult to talk about it, I wondered to myself. I said that I could appreciate how humiliated he must have felt at the time, but that this certainly was not an unheard-of experience in a child's life; we all have some such mishaps in our background; why torture himself with that memory now? He did not respond with any relief to my attempt to be helpful, nor did he have anything to add when I suggested that he continue to associate. He remained uncomfortably silent for the remainder of the session and left without saying good-bye.

Mr. Boltz did not keep his next appointment, and when I tried to reach him by phone his wife answered and said that he was not available but would get in touch with me. He never did.

## A Theory That Worked: John Washer

Years later, a situation similar to Mr. Boltz's arose with a Mr. John Washer, a depressed, forty-year-old, divorced computer programmer, in a so-called midlife crisis. He functioned effectively on his job but found that his life was lacking. He felt he was an uninterested and uninteresting person. This is the sort of complaint one often hears from people who have difficulty in the affective portion of the affective/cognitive sector of development. There was no zest or vitality to his existence, and he complained that he derived no real pleasure out of anything. Generally cooperative, he spoke of events past and present, but the sessions did not seem to lead anywhere, and Mr. Washer began repeatedly to voice doubts that he could be helped.

The following interchange took place on one occasion when he seemed at a loss for words:

THERAPIST: You are very quiet today.
MR. WASHER: I suppose so.
THERAPIST: You've noticed it too?
MR. WASHER: I guess so.
THERAPIST: How come? Any ideas . . . ?
MR. WASHER: I don't know.

THERAPIST: Don't know whether to tell me something?

MR. WASHER: *(Silence)*

THERAPIST: Is it some feeling associated with your thoughts that makes it hard to say whatever is on your mind? *(Taking my own advice, I focus the patient on his affect.)*

MR. WASHER: Yeah; I suppose . . .

THERAPIST: Which is it, fear or shame? Or am I on the wrong track?

MR. WASHER: *(Almost inaudibly)* Ashamed, I guess . . .

THERAPIST: Are these familiar thoughts or memories that you're ashamed of, or is it something new for you?

MR. WASHER: I hadn't thought about it in a long time, but on the way over here today it suddenly came in my head. I was hoping I'd forget about it before I came here so I wouldn't have to tell you.

THERAPIST: You have been wondering if you were getting anywhere here when you find yourself talking about everyday events that seem to have no particular importance. But in letting yourself just talk freely without planning what to say, or questioning anything that might occur to you, you've been getting ready to let these apparently shameful things emerge. So, paradoxically, shameful as it feels right now, this is sort of the payoff for your efforts. *(Here I enter the developmental spiral at the level of self-esteem by validating his participation in the treatment.)*

MR. WASHER: I don't want to talk about it.

THERAPIST: Of course not! Shame accompanies experiences that make us feel unacceptable. To be ashamed is to be cast into the void. Who would want openly to acknowledge something that will leave him isolated, in our case would probably cause you, as far as you are concerned, to lose my good will or respect? *(Empathy with the difficulty he is experiencing may make him feel less lonely in his shame and also permit him to go on.)*

MR. WASHER: I suppose I might as well tell you and get it over with.

THERAPIST: *(Expectant silence)*

MR. WASHER: This is awful.

THERAPIST: It can be very difficult.

MR. WASHER: I just don't know if I can. Do I have to?

THERAPIST: How do you mean?

MR. WASHER: What will happen if I don't? God, I wish I hadn't thought about it. Why did it have to come up anyway?

THERAPIST: That it's come up shows that there is a readiness to begin to deal with whatever it is, but that certainly doesn't mean it's easy. On the other hand, painful as the experience is, it has already been instructive.

MR. WASHER: How do you mean?

THERAPIST: You've been talking for a while about your lack of feeling, experiencing yourself as being devitalized and enervated. Right now there is no lack of feeling, is there? I would guess that because strong emotions or feelings are somehow wrapped up with whatever it is you dread talking about, then it makes sense that feelings of all sorts have had to be avoided, so that you won't be reminded of what it is that you don't want to think about. It's this sort of warding-off maneuver that may account for the lack of interest and excitement in your life. (*A didactic explanation of his situation, when given to a patient, often strengthens the kinship bond and provides understanding that lets him step back from the affect, so that he is able to express it.*)

MR. WASHER: You're right. I thought I just didn't want to talk about it to you, but I don't even think about it . . .

THERAPIST: You don't talk about it "in your head," so to speak, either. (*Identifying that the levels of the private and the narrative sense of self are focal here.*)

MR. WASHER: I just do it . . . (*falls silent*).

THERAPIST: (*Silent, calm, feeling that he understands the patient and that the patient feels understood.*)

MR. WASHER: I guess it makes sense to tell you—if that's what stands in the way—it can't be worse than it is . . .

THERAPIST: (*Silence*)

MR. WASHER: Well, you know, smelling stuff . . . (*in an explosive rush*) when I have a bowel movement I don't flush it down right away; I like to sit there and smell it for a while! (*Defiantly*) So there!

THERAPIST: After you've had a bowel movement, you enjoy inhaling your odors.

MR. WASHER: Maybe I made too big a fuss about it. Now that I told you, it doesn't seem that bad—not that I'm proud of it.

THERAPIST: That is often the case. Once said, much of what we imagine is so terrible doesn't sound all that bad, but that doesn't take anything away from your achievement in overcoming your understandable reluctance to talk to me about this aspect of your private life. *(Validation to restore and enhance the patient's self-esteem.)*

MR. WASHER: I never thought I could say this to anybody. It's so disgusting. I'm a very clean person. That's one of the things I never could stand about my ex; she was such a slob around the house— hair in the sink, never changed the bed—I guess I'm no better really.

THERAPIST: Fecal odors aren't inherently bad; we *learn* to despise them. As infants, stools are exciting, interesting, playworthy sorts of things. Indeed, wouldn't it be likely that the smells we generate provide some of the first clues that there is a "me," a familiar, identifying, sense-stimulating hallmark of our existence? With toilet training we learn that bowel movements are dirty and undesirable, to be disposed of quickly and privately—they become something about which we have to be ashamed. Yet, as you know from your experience, though we adopt these new rules and are offended by feces and their odor, our own products are still cherished, albeit now with a sense of shame. *(Again, a didactic explanation will not only help him to understand what happened to him and let him gain some distance but will also protect his self-esteem.)*

MR. WASHER: It doesn't sound so bad when you talk about it.

THERAPIST: Mmm.

MR. WASHER: My mother was always a fanatic about our going to the toilet. She was always knocking on the bathroom door to see what we had done . . .

In the clinical examples cited, both Mr. Boltz and Mr. Washer became aware of a secret that made them feel ashamed and, though reluctant, each managed to tell me what he was hiding. Far from helping Mr. Boltz, however, his revelation seems to have had a negative result, leading to no further associations and then to his abrupt termination of therapy. Mr. Washer, on the other hand, began to integrate and think about what he had said, coming up with associations that look as if they will lead to a deeper understanding of the situation. Yet I thought I had been no less affectively attuned to Mr. Boltz than to Mr. Washer. I not only heard what Mr. Boltz said about his bowel accident in kindergarten, I experienced within myself the sense of shame he was reliving in the session as he managed to tell me this embarrassing incident. I then tried to convey to him that the poignancy of that sort of mishap for a five- or six-year-old child was not lost upon me, but my support did not seem to do any good.

What made the difference in my therapeutic efficacy in these two cases was the theory that I had available in each case with which to organize what was going on between myself and my patient. I approached Mr. Boltz with the only organizing framework available to me then—Freud's conceptualization of development. In the absence of knowledge at that time about the psychology of infancy and childhood, Freud (1905, 1915–16, 1916–17) relied on the study of the neuroses to give him a picture of normal development. The oedipal conflict and its resolution was thought to reflect the culmination of a universal, inevitable struggle between one's instinctual heritage and society's demands that an individual's sexual and aggressive wishes be subordinated to the greater good. Two corollaries that followed were, first, that all psychopathology, not just that of the neuroses, represented an unsuccessful resolution of the basic instinctual struggle between the child and his parents; and, second, that the goal of every psychotherapy was to help the patient achieve insight into the nature of his oedipal longings and free him to direct his instinctual energies productively.

Guided by Freud's theory, I viewed what Mr. Boltz had said to me about his childhood accident as being a so-called screen memory (Freud 1914), a red herring dragged across my path by the patient's unconscious in order to divert me from the incestuous/aggressive struggle, which I assumed was what was really troubling him. After all, he must have been five or six years old when the humiliating incident occurred, a time at which a child's oedipal struggle is at its height. Verbalizing his painful secret, I anticipated, would clear the way for associations that would eventually let me help him see that the exaggerated distress over that incident really belonged to another set of experiences, probably the much more humiliating, unsuccessful attempt to capture his mother for himself. As you know, I waited in vain, and I would do so many more times with patients before our present knowledge of infant development and the centrality of affect for motivation enabled me to focus on the shame itself as the critical problem that needed to be acknowledged and worked through with the patient—an approach I took with Mr. Washer.

Patients like Mr. Boltz and Mr. Washer signal a lack of reasonable love for themselves and a depreciated self-concept. That such patients are depressed is often overlooked because they manifest neither the usual vegetative signs nor complaints of sadness or hopelessness. Instead they complain of boredom, lack of satisfaction, and the meaninglessness of their existence. This is understandable, for to become committed, enthusiastic, or hopeful exposes them to the fantasied or actual excitement about their own performance that they have learned they must eschew (see also the case of "Mr. Flynn," Basch 1988).

Using the developmental model previously outlined, I no longer had to fit Mr. Washer to the oedipal theory. Nothing he had said in his treatment at that point or before indicated a problem with sexual excitement or hostility. Accordingly, I did not focus on Mr. Washer's "anal fixation" in the hope of trying to uncover a retreat from oedipal competitiveness, but, rather, on his being ashamed of himself, and the accompanying loss of self-esteem that threatened the cohesion of his self system. I was satisfied to work with him on the level of his inchoate affect as he defended himself against coming to grips with whatever need was hidden behind his shame. Through my readiness to deal with such matters, I helped him to articulate what it was he was struggling to raise to the level of feeling. My aim was to show him that shame made sense and could be talked about to help him rekindle some hope of being understood. What would happen next I could not say. I anticipated that what we were doing would strengthen the therapeutic transference and facilitate the continued exploration of his mental life. I was prepared to examine in organized fashion whatever he might then bring up, including, of course, any oedipal or other psychosexual factors that might eventually emerge.

## Defensive Entitlement: Clarice Enpidee

One way of coping with shame is to defend against a depressing sense of worthlessness by turning it into its opposite: to insist arrogantly that one really is the center of the universe.

A person I had never seen before, Mrs. Enpidee,* called me, and in a tense, demanding voice said she needed to see me for a consultation that very day. Though I established that it was not an emergency, my

*This clinical example also appeared in Basch (1991).

explanation that I had no open appointments fell on deaf ears and only led her to reiterate her demands. The tone of her voice, and the demand that left no room for negotiation made me feel that I was being treated like a commodity.

Prior to reading Heinz Kohut's *The Analysis of the Self* (1971), I think I probably would have been both angered and speechless at being the target of such unmitigated gall. As it was, I felt a smile of recognition cross my face. Here was a pure example of what it means to be treated like a selfobject.

Believing that quite likely Mrs. Enpidee's aggressively toned air of entitlement was a cover for a fragile self and her aggression covered a sense of shame and a fear of fragmentation, I said to her that since she considered it so important to meet immediately, I would see her at the end of the day. Sounding now both injured and angry, and as if I should have known better than to offer such an appointment, she replied, "That's when I'm busy," and hung up without saying good-bye.

Experience has taught me that the aggressive attitude of entitlement manifested by people like Mrs. Enpidee is usually indicative of a frustrated kinship selfobject need. Having early on been thwarted in their wish to be treated as worthwhile members of the group, that is, by Mother or the family, these patients become first ashamed and then defensive. In Mrs. Enpidee's case, as we learned when she did eventually make an appointment and accept treatment, her depressed mother's inability to respond to her daughter, and her father's disappointment that she was not a boy created an atmosphere that, we surmised, left the child feeling isolated and unworthy of affection. Her aggressivity or, more accurately, her often inappropriate assertiveness, was both a defense against retraumatization—I don't ask; I demand and will get what I need—and a compensation for the less-than-adequate opportunity for idealizing selfobject experiences.

These insights were hard-won. For many months in therapy Mrs. Enpidee focused on my faults and shortcomings, often quite accurately and painfully, and only as I continued to hold up reasonably well and managed to keep her needs in mind, did she form an idealizing transference and trust me to care for and about her. It was only then that the aggressive posture gave way to reveal the shame behind it: the fear that she was worthless and that the more she needed me, the more likely it was that I would reject her. As this did not happen, a mirror transference could form; that is, she could look to me for approval and validation of her worth as a person.

When Mrs. Enpidee's treatment was concluded, she did not cease to need other people, but no longer ashamed of what she now understood to be perfectly legitimate longings for acceptance, support, and validation, she was able to search out appropriate opportunities to meet these needs rather than desperately demanding instant gratification. She was also now able in many situations to use her sensitivity to attune herself to others and gained considerable satisfaction from responding to their emotional requirements. When she found herself haughty, enraged, or demanding, she was usually able to recognize this attitude as a reaction to her exquisite vulnerability to being shamed and to make a fairly quick recovery. Cleverly and effectively, she would use self-deprecating humor by way of apology to make amends to whomever she had offended (see also Goldberg 1973).

## Affective Growth Through Parenthood:
## Lenore Bell

As previously discussed, shame becomes problematic when it designates as unworthy not a particular action but the individual himself. Infants, for example, who excitedly communicate affect only to be rebuffed and/or misunderstood time and time again may become ashamed of affective experiences generally and may learn to abort as quickly as possible not only the expression, but the arousal of affect. Shyness, a corollary of shame, serves as an avoidance mechanism, which is used to protect oneself from the interpersonal situations that, it is anticipated, will evoke painful affect.

The following case illustrates dramatically what is not at all uncommon—albeit not usually so extreme—in many of our patients, namely, a block to the search for competence in one or more sectors of development based on the fear of shame.

The patient, whom I will call Mrs. Bell, was a thirty-four-year-old attorney who came on the advice of her minister. She became pregnant when contraceptive measures failed, and her baby was due in three months. Her husband was ecstatic; he had wanted her to have a child ever since they were married six years previously. She had resisted the idea, citing her wish to have her career more firmly launched, wanting to accumulate more money so that she would feel more secure before starting a family, and coming up with new rationalizations for postponing children each time one of these so-called problems was solved. In fact, although she, too, had experienced within her an urge for children, she feared that she could not be a mother because for many years she had known that something made her different from other people. They seemed to use words that made sense to them but had no meaning for her, even though she had learned to use those words when necessary. When her husband, out of town on a business trip, for example, called her and said things like, "I really miss you," she had learned that the right answer was "I miss you, too." She had no inkling, however, of what that really meant—what it felt like to long for another person. And it turned out, this gap also applied to other feelings. She did not know what it was to be happy, excited, sad, or worried: feelings were a mystery to her.

Puzzled and frightened by what had happened to her, Mrs. Bell was very much aware that the complex facade of normalcy that she had created could not withstand the demands of being a mother. She was sure that she did not want her offspring to have the sort of life that she had resigned herself to leading; yet she knew no other way to live.

Pertinent aspects of her history were the following: She was the youngest of three sisters born two years apart. Her parents were high school physical education instructors, now retired. As far as food, shelter, medical attention, and general comforts went, she and her sisters were well cared for. However, her parents expressed no interest in her activities or those of her sisters. Very little discussion took place among family members; words were used to give directions or to enforce discipline. Mrs. Bell's parents were conscientious about their work and about keeping themselves and the home neat and clean, and the children were expected to follow suit, which they did.

In response to an implicit expectation, all three girls went to college and became professionals; the patient is the only one of the sisters who has married. Mrs. Bell did not know why she became an attorney. No one ever talked to her about her career choice and she did many things for the flimsiest of reasons. Someone happened to tell her, for example, that such and such a university was a good one, and she said to herself, "Ok, that's where I'll go," and she did. Mrs. Bell, in keeping with a pattern of avoiding human interaction whenever possible, chose an esoteric aspect of corporate tax law that kept her in the law library much of the time and minimally in contact with clients.

Serendipitously, the man who was to become her husband was one of the few clients that she had to deal with—a man a few years her senior, an extroverted, charming executive, who pursued her ardently with little cooperation from her. She agreed to marry him, she thought, because on some level she hoped that he would change her life, make her more like him. Although they get along well, she has not become like him, but instead, uses him as a shield between herself and the world. He is the life of the party while she sits quietly by, going through the motions she knows are expected of her.

She herself had very little knowledge about psychotherapy, but her husband, seeing her increasingly worried and anxious as the pregnancy progressed, suggested that she consult her minister, who in turn had sent her to see me.

MRS. BELL: Do you think I'm depressed? That's what Roger (the minister) thought might be the problem.

THERAPIST: Doesn't sound like it. Depression signals a retreat, a having given up on trying to deal with a situation that's overwhelming. You are still looking for solutions and appear quite able to cooperate actively. . . . No, I think if I had to hang a label on what's going on, I'd say you were anxious. That is, aware of the problem, searching yourself for some answers, but frustrated and worried that you won't be able to come up with anything that will work. Your baby will be coming shortly, and you're worried you won't be able to take care of it . . .

MRS. BELL: (Quite sharply) No, that's not the case. I can learn that. I can learn anything. We have a baby nurse coming in and I will watch what she does—that's enough.

THERAPIST: You plan to keep the nurse?

MRS. BELL: There'll be daytime help. I plan to go back to work eventually anyway. But I've done enough reading to know that babies follow their mothers' lead—it's what I do with her that will make the difference.

THERAPIST: So you know it will be a little girl.

MRS. BELL: Yes, ultrasound. Everything is normal. But so am I, on the outside. I can learn to take care *of* a baby; it's caring *about* a baby that worries me. I don't want her to be like me . . . *(At this point, though her facial expression remains bland and pleasant, tears well up and start running down her face.)* Now what's that all about? I must be more upset than I realize.

THERAPIST: Yes, it *looks* that way, but as you have explained, you don't *feel* it.

MRS. BELL: How come? Everybody else can do it—no problem.

THERAPIST: No, everybody else doesn't, at least not all the time. It's a rare person who does not have some handicap in expressing and using feelings. It's just that your situation is more global. How that happened, I don't know. But *what* happened, apparently, is that you didn't learn to feel when you should have and after a while learned to get along without it. That's what I did with mathematics: I can't do much beyond arithmetic, so I compensate, work around it, don't engage in activities where I'll need to think that way. You've done it with feeling—or, technically and more broadly speaking, with your affective life. The most important thing that people do with each other is communicate affectively, and, as we know, you've chosen an aspect of your profession in which it is possible pretty much to avoid people contact.

MRS. BELL: I thought of being a doctor for a while. I probably would have been a pathologist.

THERAPIST: Exactly.

MRS. BELL: What do I do now? You can get along without calculus; somebody else can teach that to your kids. But if what was supposed to happen naturally didn't happen to me . . .

The patient's symptoms, her history, and her present functioning—all point to a developmental arrest, what Freud (1915b), not quite accurately, called "primal repression" (Basch 1988). This is a situation in which parents, for whatever reasons, unconsciously avoid dealing with certain topics—in Mrs. Bell's case, the affective nuances of life—leaving a gap in development, which later may make itself felt as a significant handicap in the search for competence.

That Mrs. Bell picked up on my analogy between lack of affect and my block for mathematics is an important indicator of her capacity for kinship. It has been my experience that a hallmark of borderline patients is their inability to meet that selfobject need and that their impulsivity and/or anger results from frustration in trying to connect. Unable to experience kinship, the borderline patient cannot make use of the therapist's analogies—the attempts to show that despite the difference in circumstances, a sharing of basic attitudes makes empathic understanding possible. Fortunately, this little experiment revealed that Mrs. Bell's lack of affect was not an indicator of an even more serious, borderline difficulty (see also Basch 1980, 1988).

Not only was the potential for kinship present, Mrs. Bell's history indicated that her idealizing needs had been met by her parents and that there had apparently been enough mirroring to let her use her skills and talents. My approach was therefore to build on those assets and undo the developmental arrest by expanding the core self to include affective capabilities. Offering the support of an idealizing transference, I prepared to enter the developmental spiral at the behavioral level—examining and discussing her concerns about, and transactions with, her baby. This belated upbringing, or *Nacherziehung* as Freud called it, is often successful with patients like Mrs. Bell, in whom development has been arrested but whose needs have not become a source of shame and an object of defense (figure 5.1, p. 85).

MRS. BELL: *(Continuing)* Maybe I should never have told Cad *(her husband Cadwallader)* I was pregnant, and just gone ahead and gotten an abortion. *(Here, again, tears spring to her eyes. She dries them, irritably, and blows her nose.)* Damn . . .

THERAPIST: I did not say that affective awareness and acquiring the capacity for useful affective communication are "natural," that they just happen. Quite the contrary; they're learned, and you just told me you can learn anything.

MRS. BELL: Who's going to teach me?

THERAPIST: I will. And of course so will your daughter.

MRS. BELL: Where do we start?

THERAPIST: At the beginning—yours, mine, your little girl's, everybody's. Think of your brain as a supercomplex computer that comes into the world not quite fully programmed. When the pediatrician tells you . . . by the way, do you have a name for your baby yet?

MRS. BELL: Heather, after Cad's favorite sister . . .

THERAPIST: You like the choice?

MRS. BELL: I didn't have any; he wanted it, so I told him it was fine with me. Do you think it's a good name for a girl?

THERAPIST: Sounds like a sweet name to me. "Heather Bell," that goes well together. Is she going to have a middle name?

MRS. BELL: "Cadwallader," my husband's mother's maiden name.

THERAPIST: "Heather Cadwallader Bell"—very elegant. Is your husband from the South?

MRS. BELL: Very much so. I think we'd be living in Atlanta if it weren't for his business. He's always involved with his family, and all the aunts and uncles . . .

THERAPIST: And you and your family?

MRS. BELL: I see my parents once a month maybe, but there's never much to say. I've nothing against them; it's just . . . well, you know, once you say, "I'm fine, and Cad's fine," and "How are you?" and they are fine, that's pretty much it. Aunts and uncles I see at weddings and funerals.

THERAPIST: And your sisters?

MRS. BELL: We were never that close. Anyway, they're in California. We talk on the phone once in a while. But you were saying something about the pediatrician . . .

THERAPIST: Oh, yes. When the pediatrician tells you that Heather is a healthy little girl and that you can take her home, what he is saying is that, as far as he can ascertain, all the computer's—the brain's—hardwired programs for controlling things like temperature, blood pressure, breathing, digestion, and so on, are functioning well, and that you can expect further development will proceed uneventfully. What he isn't telling you, because we all take it for granted, is that the kind of little girl Heather will be is not something foreordained. After some months your doctor can pretty much predict how tall Heather will be when she reaches adulthood, but how she will feel about herself—that is an open question. Oh, there are a lot of things that relate to future personality and social adjustment that are already present at birth—every nurse in the newborn nursery will tell you that each baby from day one can be identified by its particular temperament, as expressed in its crying and other behavior; and talents of various sorts, like musical ability, for instance, certainly seem to have a strong inherited component—but how Heather's inherent potential will become structured as her character, her self, is open to the influence of the environment and—just as you intimated—here, although I don't want to minimize the significance of a participating father, the influence of the mother in those first twenty-four months is of paramount importance.

MRS. BELL: In other words, you've got to program the computer?

THERAPIST: That's what happens.

MRS. BELL: How does that happen? They can't talk or think yet. How do you know what to do?

THERAPIST: There is a tendency to think about thinking in verbal terms. Babies don't use words, but in their own way they "talk," and they certainly think. Thinking consists of generating information and using it to come to decisions about behavior. Babies do that. Once they like something, they tend to repeat it, and if they find it painful, they try to avoid it. How is that any different from what we do? And babies talk; they don't use words, but they do use facial expressions accompanied by sounds and movements to indicate discomfort, pleasure, and interest. Words fine-tune communication later, but basically that's also what we do as adults: communicate how we feel about what is going on in our lives, and, based on the kind of return we get, form patterns of expectation that act like maps in guiding future behavior.

MRS. BELL: So if I teach Heather to talk that way she'll be okay?

THERAPIST: You don't have to teach her. Heather will be born prepared to talk to you affectively; you will be the one to learn how to respond to her. In this way you will recapture what you had when you were little that was somehow lost along the way.

MRS. BELL: What's lesson number one?

THERAPIST: We've already had it—an orientation to what's going on in a baby's brain that bears on her psychological development.

MRS. BELL: I wonder what happened to me?

THERAPIST: I don't know. Some things happened that resulted in your having to back away from your affects; that's what we're not going to let happen to Heather.

MRS. BELL: You think it's doable?

THERAPIST: Yes, I do. You've been open with me and cooperative with the process. Keep that up and I'll take care of my end. Let's get something set up for next week.

In subsequent sessions Mrs. Bell and I had a chance to explore her background and current functioning in greater detail. It became clear that, far from being affectless, one affect governed her life, and that was shame. I explained to Mrs. Bell, much as I began to do at the start of this chapter, that shame is a perfectly useful experience. Shame is the inner response we often experience when the response we anticipate and/or hope for is not forthcoming. When we expect open arms and instead are rebuffed, the autonomic vascular reaction that makes us feel uncomfortably warm is a sign that our excitement will not be shared and thereby relieved, and a signal to stop trying to get that response. In other words, shame, in making us feel bad about what we are trying to do, stops us from making even bigger fools of ourselves; it is a protective mechanism.

Feeling less than worthy in a particular situation is one thing; however, shame about one's own affective reactions and a sense of worthlessness for being oneself is another. When a baby's affective signals do not elicit a response, then a state of painful tension, shame, is created. Eventually, seeking to avoid a repetition of unrequited excitement, the baby learns to stifle its affective responses. Like an autoimmune reaction, the baby becomes allergic to its own affect—turns it off as quickly as possible and learns to avoid situations that generate it. This, as I hypothesized to Mrs. Bell, may well have happened to her. She, of course, had no recollection of her infancy and, as is often the case with patients who have suffered this sort of trauma, had very few memories of her childhood. Children who have an antipathy to their own affect have a sense of humiliation as their constant companion and make an effort to defend themselves by saying, "Nothing matters." And what does not matter is not remembered.

As we were talking about these issues, Mrs. Bell recalled the following episodes, which underscored for both of us how the fear of shame undermined her affective development.

Even though her parents were physical education instructors, she had never had swimming lessons as a child. During the summer she often went to the beach by herself. But by that time she held herself apart. She wanted friends but could not bring herself to seek out peers; Put off by her aloofness, they largely ignored her. On one of these solitary excursions to the lake-front, when she was about twelve years old, she went into the water intending to remain close to shore where her feet touched bottom. Other children playing in the water splashed water in her eyes;

her vision obscured, she stumbled toward what she thought was the beach and did not realize she was heading in the wrong direction. Suddenly she found herself in water over her head. Unable to swim, she began to flail about, trying to bounce back to safety, but could not get a foothold on the lake's bottom. As she tried to elevate herself above the water's surface to get air, she caught glimpses of people who, being tall enough, were walking around near her. At that moment she knew two things: that she was going to drown, and that death was preferable to letting her need be known and calling for help.

Just then, two strong hands lifted her under her armpits and moved her a foot or two nearer to the shore where she was safe. The man who saved her life said something; she did not hear the words but thought his tone of voice was kind. This made things even worse for her; she was too ashamed to thank him and instead turned away, brusquely throwing herself into the shallow water and pretending she could swim. Far from being either relieved or grateful, she felt terribly humiliated. Lo and behold, as she pretended to be swimming, she found that her dog-paddling movements were keeping her from sinking. By the time she left the beach that afternoon, she had taught herself to swim well enough to forestall a repetition of her embarrassment earlier in the day.

The second incident occurred when she began her professional career. Before going to her office, Mrs. Bell would stop at a particular restaurant for breakfast and, since she was a regular customer and always ordered the same thing, the waitress would say, "Hello," and automatically get her breakfast ready for her. This pattern was interrupted when Mrs. Bell went on a two-week vacation. On her return, the waitress said to her, "Oh, we missed you; where have you been? I hope you weren't sick. Did you go on a trip?" The patient answered her politely but changed restaurants the next day. It had become too anxiety-provoking. She hadn't realized she was more than a breakfast to the waitress; she had become a person, a target for emotions, and this was too much for her. To be singled out provided an occasion for experiencing shame, and the fear of shame necessitated that she remove herself from that situation, as she had from so many others where affect might be aroused.

In analyzing such patients, one often discovers a longing to be responded to, which is accompanied by a conviction that one's need either will not be recognized or will be rebuffed. The anticipated humiliation is so painful that a pathologic shyness, like Mrs. Bell's, serves as a superimposed defense to preclude this scenario's playing itself out.

I explained to Mrs. Bell that she would find herself, as the mother of a newborn baby, the target of the most intense affect that any of us experience, and that we would work not only to make her responsive to her child but to help her learn to enjoy this potentially rewarding relationship. I said to her, "We're going to have a great opportunity. When that baby is born you're going to be experiencing things that you and I are going to be talking about. You and your baby are going to grow up together in ways that you never had a chance to do before." And that is essentially what happened. I will recount here only a few telling examples of how the patient undid the affective arrest from which she had suffered so long.

Mrs. Bell was worried at first that she was doing something wrong when she fed Heather, because the baby gazed intently at her face with what seemed to be a very serious expression, and did not smile. I explained to the patient that Heather was displaying interest, that the pleasant, nonstressful feeding situation gave Heather a chance to take in her mother's face and connect it with the satisfying and calm situation in which she found herself. These "lived moments" (Stern 1985) in which the combination of experiencing a need, the activity employed in satisfying the need, and the affect attached to the experience are recorded in memory, are the fundamental units for character formation. They become the basis for the increasingly complex patterns of expectation with which the infant meets the environment. I had Mrs. Bell observe how, for example, Heather at first cried bitterly when she woke up hungry at night, and how she would not quiet down until the bottle was in her mouth. But it was not long before the parent's footstep, or the turning on of the light in the room, served to quiet her down. As indicated by her behavior, Heather had learned to substitute happy anticipation for distress once the opening moves of the feeding-at-night sequence were initiated. In this way Mrs. Bell became comfortable with Heather's progress as she saw the baby daily mastering all sorts of activities.

Mrs. Bell was amazed by how friendly Heather was. Our discussion of a baby's affective life had prepared Mrs. Bell for what was happening, but to experience it was another matter. Several times she found herself crying for no apparent reason when she held the baby, and she wanted to know whether this was going to be bad for the child. I explained to her that tears were sort of an "emotional sweating," a sign of intense affective activity, but not necessarily anything negative. Quite probably, I suggested, she was crying from excitement and joy—not only happy to be caring for her baby, but happy to be feeling differently about herself. Heather would experience her mother's crying for what it was, a positive affective response to their being together. "How can she tell?" Mrs. Bell wanted to know. I reminded her of an earlier conversation in which Mrs. Bell had noted that when one baby was distressed and cried in the newborn nursery, soon all the babies took up the chant. At that time she had wanted to know why babies imitated each other that way. I had explained to her that this was not imitation; imitation requires skills that a newborn does not possess. (In humans, imitation is a product of cortical functioning—a voluntary reflective act. Affect is processed subcortically and automatically.) In the nursery babies become "infected" with each other's affect; that is, looking at a distressed face or hearing a cry of distress causes the baby to generate automatically within itself the same affect—a state to which it then responds. When baby number one cries in distress, therefore, baby number two becomes distressed and cries, as a result of experiencing what has now become this second baby's dysphoria. Similarly, when a mother, overcome by tender feelings, cries as she holds the baby, the child generates within herself the same positive ambience. Indeed, babies, much more accurately than our adult peers, experience exactly how we feel and are unerringly alert to the nuances and changes in our feelings.

Some time later I reminded Mrs. Bell of this interchange. She had been making good progress, getting along very well with Heather, and was now receiving enormous pleasure from the affective interchange with the baby. One week, however, she reported that Heather was fussy and distressed when she fed her, whereas when her father fed her, she was her usual interested, animated self. We could not figure out what was going on until I asked the patient what she was thinking about while feeding Heather. It turned out that about the time that Heather became fussy with her, Mrs. Bell, who had taken a leave of absence from her firm, had been contacted by one of her partners who needed to ask her some questions about a mutual client. As had been her habit, Mrs. Bell focused on that problem to the exclusion of everything else. Consequently, her thoughts were on the client's problems even while she was feeding the baby. Heather immediately responded to this situation. Her mother's mood was contrary to what she had learned to expect at mealtime. This change, compounded by the stress created when the baby had to seek stimulation to compensate for the boredom of a mechanical feeding, generated distress and anger—the fussy crying being a signal for mother to rectify the situation. Following my explanation, Mrs. Bell focused her interest on Heather when they were together, and within hours she restored the normal harmony between herself and her baby.

Mrs. Bell's concern about her capacity for motherhood gave way to a comfortable relationship in which she became increasingly aware of her affective responses and the feelings that these indicated. When Heather was about nine months old, Mr. Bell, who had made a concerted effort to avoid business trips in order to be with his wife and the baby, had to leave town for a few days. Mrs. Bell told me that for the first time she experienced what it meant to miss someone and long for his return.

Shortly thereafter, Mrs. Bell quite spontaneously began to pay attention to how her parents interacted with the baby. Her father tried to be an affectionate grandparent, but held Heather gingerly as if he expected her to soil him at any moment. Her mother, once satisfied that Heather was well fed and growing normally, seemed to have little interest in playing with the baby. Unlike other grandmothers, whom Mrs. Bell had met in the park when taking Heather for her daily airing, her mother did not talk about the baby but preferred to converse about other topics. At first Mrs. Bell was angry and hurt by this, but then she began to treat her parents' disinterest as a puzzle to be solved. She tried to talk to her parents about her own childhood but did not get very far. She did obtain from them some home movies and photographs taken when she was a baby and a little girl, and saw herself as very different from Heather: not nearly as smiling or animated, she thought of herself as lonely and depressed in these films.

Eventually she hit upon talking to her parents about their respective childhoods and was surprised to find them responding positively. Both of her parents had been raised in a pietistic community where worldly concerns, as well as preoccupation with oneself, were frowned upon. Her parents thought of emotional displays as "spoiling" children, and raised the patient and her sisters on a very short affective leash. It seemed clear that though her parents had rebelled against the religious aspect of their upbringing, running away to elope when they were only teenagers, they carried over its emotionally restrictive attitudes into their own parenting activities. Interestingly, as Mrs. Bell succeeded in her efforts to know her parents better, the older people's affective set changed in significant ways. As her husband remarked to Mrs. Bell, her parents were becoming quite human. They began to visit more often and stayed longer, and in their own clumsy but now endearing fashion let themselves enjoy their grandchild.

It was instructive to see in retrospect how a particular restrictive affective set had been carried from one generation to the next, and it was very gratifying to see three generations—to say nothing of those to come if Heather eventually has children—benefit from the knowledge we have today about normal development.

My work with Mrs. Bell illustrates an important aspect of affective communication. As therapeutic technique based on the traditional psychoanalytic model is usually outlined—and as Freud (1916–17) was the first to teach—treatment follows the developmental sequence. First we engage the patients' affect; then through clarification and interpretation of their emotions, we help them to understand themselves cognitively. But what Mrs. Bell's case illustrates dramatically holds true at least to some extent in most cases we see in psychotherapy, namely, that a patient's affective immaturity, distortion, or conflict, precludes that approach. Then it is important to remember that, though initially it is the affective aspect of experience that forms the nidus around which cognition coalesces, once cognitive capacity has matured and we have the power to generate experience cortically, rather than having to rely only on external stimuli to do so, then it is possible to reverse the developmental sequence. Using didactic explanation to involve the patient, we are able to mobilize affect that, having been disavowed, has not evolved into feelings and emotions appropriate for adult life (Basch 1983a, 1988).

# CHAPTER 5

---

## *Dealing with Anger*

---

A QUESTION I AM MOST FREQUENTLY ASKED in conferences and workshops pertains to how I deal with the initially aggressive or hostile patient. A few years ago Dr. James P. Lynch, a participant in a workshop conducted by Dr. Robert Mark and myself, volunteered, using clinical material familiar to him, to play the part of the hostile patient and give me a chance to respond as I would in an initial interview with such a person—a man whom I will call Theodore Bear. Although we were role-playing, Dr. Lynch's skill was so fine-tuned that within seconds we were affectively engaged in the encounter. First I will present the transcript; then I will describe my thought processes as I worked with "Mr. Bear" and strove to become empathic with what he was communicating.

## The Initial Interview

MR. BEAR: I had a hell of a time getting here . . . couldn't find a fucking meter. How much does it cost to park in that shit lot?

THERAPIST: Where is your car?

MR. BEAR: *(Grudgingly, but in a less angry tone of voice)* In the lot across the street.

THERAPIST: About seven-fifty, I imagine.

MR. BEAR: So, I don't know. . . . Crap. . . . I'm already about twenty minutes late?

THERAPIST: Yeah, about twenty minutes late.

MR. BEAR: You think it's worth it to get into anything? Should I just make another appointment?

THERAPIST: Let's go ahead, as long as you're here, let's see what we can get done.

MR. BEAR: I don't remember what I told you on the phone. I think I told you about being real angry and that my boss said I should come here. That's all. So here I am.

THERAPIST: Well, why don't you tell me some of the incidents that made your boss decide this for you.

MR. BEAR: I had an explosion, kind of, at work . . . construction work. I do elevator construction, and I got this helper that I can't fucking stand. I want to say . . . it's been getting worse, and it gave me kind of an excuse for just finally blowing up at him, but not like this. . . . I was trying to throw him off the building. There were other people around, and I just lost it, I just fucked up.

THERAPIST: What provoked you so much? What is it about him that riles you so, if you can identify it?

MR. BEAR: He just took too long on his coffee break . . . I don't know if you know what it's like, but the helper kind of fetches for you. And he was just taking too long. I mean, he didn't have this coming to him. But, I mean, this incident is not the only one . . . I've been doing this a lot. . . .

THERAPIST: With this man?

MR. BEAR: No, I can't predict. . . . I've just really got a short fuse.

THERAPIST: When did you start noticing this? Is it a lifelong characteristic that you have such a short fuse and can't predict when you'll explode, or is it something that's developed recently?

MR. BEAR: Well, it's kind of been spilling all over, the last three or four months, but if I'm really honest about it . . . a long time.

THERAPIST: Since you were ten years old? Since you were a teenager? Even when you were a little boy?

MR. BEAR: Oh yeah, absolutely. I think it was when I was about seven; I came home from school and I was so proud. My class had voted me the most sarcastic. I told my father. I didn't know what the word meant. And he said, it's nothing to be proud of. I remember that.

THERAPIST: Did your father explain to you what sarcastic meant?

MR. BEAR: I don't remember. I just remember that he told me it was nothing to be proud of.

THERAPIST: When you think about it, were you sort of a sarcastic child? I'm not so sure myself of the dictionary definition of sarcastic. . . .

MR. BEAR: Not giving a shit what people think. If that's sarcastic, I guess . . . I just think I was showing off.

THERAPIST: Even in second grade you didn't give a shit what people thought?

MR. BEAR: No. I pretty much was on my own, looking out for myself. Didn't bother me. I didn't have a lot of friends, but that's okay too.

THERAPIST: It worked, I guess, up to a point, because apparently you got along. You got an important job; you're making a reasonable living, and it worked okay until now when . . .

MR. BEAR: Real important job! I hate my fucking work.

THERAPIST: Well, I guess that's sarcastic when you say, "Real important job!" That's the sarcasm, sort of belittling yourself now. But in any case, that's the work that you're doing, and your character— your personality—let you get to this point as a loner, taking care of yourself. It almost sounds as if this blow-up with your helper, when he took that long coffee break . . . in a sense, he wasn't looking out for you; he wasn't a helper at all. By taking that time, he wasn't thinking about you . . .

MR. BEAR: Oh crap. How the fuck long do you figure this is going to take, this whole thing? Do I have to come again?

THERAPIST: Well, I think it's got to be an open-ended kind of thing. You're telling me about a problem that is now, sort of, blowing up on you, at your age. . . . How old are you now?

MR. BEAR: Forty-nine.

THERAPIST: Forty-nine. You're now forty-nine years old. Something that has been going on ever since you were a little boy is now threatening to overwhelm you and get you into some real difficulties with others and, I would imagine, with yourself. So when you say, "How long is this going to take?" I sure can't tell you. But let's say . . . you're forty-nine years old . . . let's say we have forty-nine appointments and then see where we're going, one appointment for each year.

MR. BEAR: Excuse me . . . forty-nine appointments?

THERAPIST: Forty-nine appointments—and then let's see where we are.

MR. BEAR: I'm not crazy about this one. How'm I going to last through forty-nine of 'em?

THERAPIST: Well, you know, I didn't mean it's got to be forty-nine exactly. Just that this is going to take some time and we've got to give it the time it takes. You've got a lot at stake, and it's not necessarily something that you have to live with for the rest of your life. . . .

MR. BEAR: I've been living with it so far. I'm just interested in putting a cap on this bullshit.

THERAPIST: Well, let's try to do that.

MR. BEAR: I don't feel like I need to, you know, go back into my childhood. That's past history, you know.

THERAPIST: Not in your case it isn't. I think it's very much with you, although I'm perfectly willing to stick with the present. What else do you want to tell me about what is going on in your life now?

MR. BEAR: I don't know. I need to know some of these things to do in order to just not explode any more.

THERAPIST: Well, I think you got two possibilities. I don't know enough about you to tell you what to do. One thing that you could do is you could take a leave of absence from your work and just work on this for a while . . .

MR. BEAR: Who pays the rent if I do that? It's not some fancy job where you can call in sick. I'm no banker or nothin'. I don't get paid if I'm not there.

THERAPIST: Well, then I think you should be coming here and working on this because, otherwise, as you say, "Who pays the rent?" The way you're going it's possible that you won't have any job at all. I think otherwise you wouldn't be here.

MR. BEAR: God dam' right I wouldn't be here if the boss didn't tell me to come.

THERAPIST: Right, and your job is at stake, and maybe you can't get another one, so, I don't know if . . .

MR. BEAR: Okay, I'm here, aren't I?

THERAPIST: Okay. So you're here and I'm here, and since . . . I don't see what your choice is. Either I can help you or I can't, and if I can't, you're in real trouble. So I would say, let's try it. Why are you shaking your head?

MR. BEAR: Because I don't have a fucking choice, do I?

THERAPIST: I don't think so. And for a loner, that's not an easy situation to be in, to come to see a stranger who says, "Hey, you've got to trust me and maybe I can help you . . . at least I hope so." It's not an easy thing to do. But as you say, you don't have much choice.

MR. BEAR: So what do we do?

THERAPIST: Keep on going. If you keep talking, you'll let me know what I need to know about you in order to understand you. Don't make any decisions about "this is unimportant, and that's none of his business, and that doesn't matter"; just say what you're thinking about yourself to me. What do I need to know to understand you? Right now all I know is that you're forty-nine years old and you've been angry for most of those years, and it's catching up with you—and you hate your job, but you need it. Is that all there is to you?

MR. BEAR: I don't know.

THERAPIST: What does that mean, you don't know? What don't you know?

MR. BEAR: I don't know what to say.

THERAPIST: Well, then that's the first thing that we have to do . . .

MR. BEAR: I know, I don't like . . . I hate it when I have to do what I *have* to do.

THERAPIST: All right, you don't have to *like* being here. It's like your job. You say you hate your job; you don't like your job either, but you gotta do it, because otherwise you don't have anything to support you, and apparently the alternative to working is not one that you want to accept. And in the same way, your being here is not something you have to like; it's something you need.

MR. BEAR: Okay, okay, so I need to be here—there's something else that happened.

THERAPIST: Okay.

MR. BEAR: I have a three-year-old son . . .

THERAPIST: Mmmm.

MR. BEAR: . . . and I told him to do something the other day and he didn't do it. And I told him again and he laughed at me. And I picked him up and I threw him on the couch. That's the first time I'd ever done anything like that.

THERAPIST: Mmmm.

MR. BEAR: He wasn't hurt.

THERAPIST: But you were.

MR. BEAR: I didn't like what I did.

THERAPIST: Would you say you were frightened by what you did, or that you were ashamed, or both? What would you say the feeling was?

MR. BEAR: Yeah, yeah. I know that can't happen again.

THERAPIST: You say you never did anything like that. You mean you never had to discipline or punish your son before?

MR. BEAR: I'm a fucking child abuser. That's the way I feel.

THERAPIST: That's not what I asked you. What I asked you was, haven't you . . . this is a three-year-old kid; you mean you never had to discipline him before?

MR. BEAR: Sure, but I've never put a hand on him.

THERAPIST: How do you discipline him? What kind of things would he do, and how did you handle it?

MR. BEAR: I just put him in his room, or I would hold him, let him cry, holler at him. I just lost it.

THERAPIST: And this episode with your son preceded what happened with the helper? It came a couple of months earlier, a week . . . ?

MR. BEAR: This was a month ago.

THERAPIST: And with the helper, when did it happen?

MR. BEAR: Last week.

THERAPIST: So, anything else that went wrong for you?

MR. BEAR: I'm just tense all the time, all the time.

THERAPIST: Yes, I can see that, that's probably true.

MR. BEAR: And I feel like I'm waitin' for somebody to piss me off, like I'm looking for an opportunity. You piss me off.

THERAPIST: What did I do that pisses you off?

MR. BEAR: I mean . . . nothing . . . you know? *Being there.* Your asking me questions about my feelings; I don't want to talk about my feelings. I want you to give me a pill or something, or a prescription. I just want it fixed. I want it to go away.

THERAPIST: Wish I could. But I don't believe this is a situation where pills are going to help you. I don't think you have the kind of problem that pills will do anything for, and I think this is going to have to be worked on by doing what you don't want to do, which is talking about yourself, including the feelings. But I think we have one thing that's really going for us and I am very encouraged by it, which is that you're honest. You know, you're telling me what you're thinking and what you're feeling, and you don't hesitate to tell me how you feel about me. I think that's exactly what we need, that you say what you're thinking.

Mr. Bear: Oh, I will do that.

Therapist: That's all I'm asking you to do, to say what you're thinking—about yourself, about this situation, about your life.

Mr. Bear: But I can't promise you that I'm going to stick out forty-nine sessions.

Therapist: Well, maybe . . .

Mr. Bear: I've never done anything like this before and I don't talk to anybody about me.

Therapist: I think that's one of the big problems.

Mr. Bear: I feel like it's my business.

Therapist: What about your wife?

Mr. Bear: Yeah. We talk, once in a while.

Therapist: But you don't talk about yourself. Is that your business? You don't talk to your wife about your feelings, how you felt about throwing your son on the couch?

Mr. Bear: She doesn't know.

Therapist: What *do* you talk to your wife about?

Mr. Bear: We talk, you know . . . we talk about family, we talk about . . .

Therapist: Do you talk about the tension that you feel constantly?

Mr. Bear: No, we talk about her feelings.

Therapist: Do you talk about the job that you don't like?

Mr. Bear: Yeah, yeah, that we do. She knows I don't like it.

Therapist: How does she respond?

Mr. Bear: How does she respond? We've got bills.

Therapist: You make it sound like you feel she spends too much or spends on things you can't afford.

Mr. Bear: Nah, she's a good woman.

Therapist: How long have you been married?

Mr. Bear: Ten years. The second time. My first wife was a real asshole. So was I.

Therapist: How long were you divorced before you got married?

Mr. Bear: Two years.

Therapist: You think you made the right choice this time?

MR. BEAR: I love her. I'm the problem.

THERAPIST: Do you think she loves you?

MR. BEAR: Well, I don't know. I ain't too lovable. She cares for me, takes care of me. She's good.

THERAPIST: But, in spite of it, you feel constantly tense and ready to explode.

MR. BEAR: You got it.

THERAPIST: Okay, we've made a good start, I think. Let's stop for today, and make another appointment. Today is Monday; is Friday at three possible for you?

MR. BEAR: It'll be all right.

THERAPIST: Think you can handle it till then—stay in control?

MR. BEAR: I won't kill anybody, if that's what you mean.

THERAPIST: Or yourself?

MR. BEAR: Naw—that'd make too many people happy.

THERAPIST: See you Friday.

## Analysis of the Initial Interview

Initially, I was taken aback by the patient's nasty, challenging tone: ". . . couldn't find a fucking meter"—as if I were to blame for the difficulty he had parking his car. At the same time, it struck me how much of a little boy he was. "How much does it cost to park in that shit lot?" What lot? I work in downtown Chicago and am surrounded by parking lots. Very much like a child who announces that he is going to his friend's house and expects that you, of course, know which of his pals he means, Mr. Bear expected me to know what lot he was talking about.

My voice matter-of-fact, I now ask a question meant to orient both of us: "Where is your car?" My tone sends a message that I will, at least at this point, not make an issue of his anger, that is, I will not reproach him nor react in kind. By not responding apologetically, however, to the implication that because of the location of my office I am somehow guilty of inconveniencing him and upsetting him, I also signal that I will not take the blame for his difficulty.

If he is able to hear the affective nuances and their implications, in the split second he needs to register my reply, he will—not necessarily consciously—understand a great deal about me and how I work. The content of my questioning also tells him that if I am to help him, he must make himself clear. If he wants me to tell him what parking costs, I have to know where he ended up. I am not averse to answering questions, but I want to know specifics before hazarding a guess. Again, if the deeper implication of what I am saying registers with him, he has learned something about me and how, if I have a choice, I structure the therapeutic relationship. What I need to know now in order to begin to orient myself to him depends on his answer, which is, "In the lot across the street."

The moment I heard his voice—still angry but not nearly as much as it had been initially—I felt encouraged. My willingness not to react to his rage in kind—showing him through the tone of my voice and my choice of words that I had not ruled out kinship, as he was daring me to do with his intemperate tone and vocabulary—had a positive effect. It is true he did not apologize, "Sorry, Doctor, but I really wanted to get here to see you, and then not finding a parking place really made me tense." To that response I would have replied, "Yes, I know, that can be awfully frustrating." But on the other hand, he did not insist on maintaining an angry stance, for example, "Ah, what the fuck's the difference where I'm parked." In telling him that parking will probably cost about seven dollars and fifty cents in that lot, I try to defuse with a matter-of-fact answer what he intended to be a challenge and an accusation. Although this again presents an opportunity for him to respond aggressively: "Oh shit, seven-fifty? Who the fuck needs to pay that?," he does not take it. Instead, a further deescalation of his anger takes place as the patient now begins to wonder whether the time lost from our appointment means that he should leave and make another one, to which he will presumably come on time. In other words, he is saying that whatever doubts regarding our proposed relationship were implied by his angry outburst were settled to his satisfaction, and he will even accept having to leave and come back on another day. He acknowledges his need to be heard. From this interchange I conclude provisionally that Mr. Bear is not as superficial and concrete in his approach to his problems as he seemed to be at first.

His response makes me hopeful that he might lend himself to an exploratory, dynamic therapeutic approach—an examination of his decision-making process that will serve as the basis for its reorganization. I also learned something else from his willingness to forgo the abbreviated appointment; namely, he recognizes limits, and he is able to see me as a person with obligations and constraints of my own. Some patients, like Mrs. Enpidee (pp. 58–60), are unable to take into account that I work on a schedule and by appointment; my time belongs to them and no needs other than their own exist.

When I agree to work with him in the time remaining to us, he comes right out with the reason for his being sent to see me. I am impressed by his straightforward manner but find myself momentarily frightened by the patient's readiness for violent behavior. I remind myself that he did not actually throw his helper from the scaffold, and I remember his recognition of the limits on time here with me. I can only imagine, given how angry the patient got when he couldn't find a parking place, what it must be like to be his helper.

I am not here to identify with the helper, however, but to understand Mr. Bear's functioning. My next question—"What provoked you so much? What is it about him that riles you so, if you can identify it?"—is consonant with the developmental theory that ultimately governs the way I work: everything a person does or says is in some way related to the search for competence and the enhancement or repair of self-esteem. From an observer's point of view, no matter how un-sane or counterproductive Mr. Bear's outburst may have been, at that moment Mr. Bear had a "good," that is, psychologically understandable, reason for what he did. Thinking in that vein, I avoided responding in a way that would threaten the kinship between the two of us, for example, "My God, how could you!?" Nor did I simply say nothing or make a bland comment like, "Well, tell me more about what happened." Any of those responses would have increased his shame, thereby also undermining kinship and probably pushing him into defensive anger toward me. By asking Mr. Bear what provoked him, accepting his behavior as in its own way reasonable, affectively displaying interest rather than contempt or disgust, I support his already sagging self-esteem. Also I start to work at the decision-making level of the pathological spiral, learning how he came to find it necessary to solve a problem in such a manner.

Although further exploration would not have been appropriate at this time, I am not overlooking that a patient's reaction to people in the present reflects, however distortedly, something from his or her past.

What memories does his helper evoke in Mr. Bear? What of Mr. Bear's past has been stirred up by his helper's conduct, appearance, or attitude? In an ongoing treatment I would expect that the opportunity for learning such things would in all probability occur.

Mr. Bear's reason for being furious with his helper is a lame rationalization: "He just took too long on his coffee break." In other words, the reason for his violent behavior is unconscious and unknown. My own affective reaction leads me to think that I can hear a little boy crying, "He left me all alone, all by myself." I am beginning to think that this man is desperate to be liked and loved but has no scripts written for achieving these goals. Furthermore, when frustrated in his search for competence, he behaves like a baby who cries and lashes out to signal his distress. The affective maturation that might let him better express his needs, longings, and disappointments is not there. Affect does not get translated into specific feelings but becomes a source of overstimulation and only gives rise to diffuse anger (Basch 1983a, 1988). When I was able to accept his anger as a signal for help, he quieted down very quickly.

As I further explore his history of explosive rage, he clearly remembers having always had "a short fuse." When he then tells a story of coming home, proudly announcing to his father that he was voted the most sarcastic in his class, I resonate affectively with the shame I assume he felt when his father deflated him, apparently without the compassion and concern to work with his son on the problem. At this point, I felt terribly sorry for Mr. Bear. Memories of my own childhood humiliations flashed through consciousness, those remembered painful episodes when I thought I was quite something, only to realize later that I had played the fool.

This leads Mr. Bear to tell me about the bitter, lonely, proud resolution that has permitted him to function ". . . on my own, looking out for myself." I validate the competent aspect of that decision by agreeing that he has achieved a lot that way but that now it is no longer enough. To myself I think how lonely this man is, how hungry for understanding and for relationships he can neither foster nor maintain.

Mr. Bear counters my comments by sarcastically downgrading what he has achieved, and I point out the sarcasm and how he belittles not just others, but himself. When I suggest to him that although he prides himself on being a loner, he also wants to be looked after and cared for and that that need explains why he blew up with his helper, the patient immediately shifts to how long treatment is going to take. I think to myself that beneath the seeming impatience and unwillingness to work out his problem is a real hope that he has found what he has been looking for. I am firm, showing him that I can be a bit sarcastic too—let's say we have forty-nine appointments, one for each year that you've been in trouble and then we'll see where we are. In my refusal to back down, I demonstrate that I will not be frightened or intimidated by him, that I understand quite well what he needs and wants, and I care enough to see that he gets a chance to reverse the self-destructive process in whose grip he finds himself.

I am not advocating the particular intervention I made: how one says things depends on one's personality and therapeutic style, but however one gets the point across, it would have been a real failure of empathy, in my opinion, to take a soft, conciliatory tone. He is frightened by emotional neediness. To indicate that I, for my sake, need to help him would frighten him further. During this time I feel increasingly calm and confident—in charge of the situation—and see it unfolding as I predicted. By emphasizing his need to help himself, I am betting that this man's good intelligence and his high functioning in the sector of autonomy will overcome his conviction that any move toward attachment will come to naught. And that is indeed what happened: "I don't have a fucking choice, do I?" This statement acknowledges the beginning transference of an idealizing need to me. Having tested me, he trusts me to be strong and knowledgeable enough to support him. In turn, I mirror, that is, validate, his decision by affirming that it is an act of courage for someone like him, a loner, to trust a relative stranger to help him.

There is a last skirmish to make sure I will not take his negativism at face value: "I hate it when I have to do what I *have* to do." I am not bothered that he does not like having to be here, and by implication that he does not like being with me, and maybe does not like me: "Your being here is not something you have to like, it's something you need." What I am also doing is relieving any pressure he feels for having to make an emotional expenditure that is not yet feasible for him: he does not have to like anything; we are dealing with need, the need of the unconscious. The patient now openly agrees: "I think I need to be here," and then tells of his rage at his three-year-old son, who laughed at him instead of obeying him.

Here again I note the delicate balance of the patient's self-esteem. It sounds to me as if he threw his son on the couch, not because the boy disobeyed him, but because he laughed, a response the patient considered a shaming, derisive commentary on his authority. The patient adds that it was the first time he ever behaved that way and that his son was not hurt. I could have said in effect, "Well, who doesn't get mad at a kid once in a while and overreact; did you apologize to him?" This would have been a supportive comment intended to help him see that his anger was not his basic problem but a reaction to it, that is, a reaction to his vulnerable and damaged sense of self. True as I believe that formulation is, I did not make it because it would have been premature and ineffective. What stands in the way of his being reassured and coming to grips with the underlying selfobject need that drives, that is motivates, his pathologic behavior is the shame that he experiences when these needs threaten to emerge and assert themselves. As figure 5.1 portrays, when attempts to fulfill a selfobject need are traumatically rejected or ignored, a person becomes ashamed of his need. This means that whenever an occasion arises that might evoke that particular need, there is an anticipation of shame—a dreadful sense of worthlessness that must be avoided at all cost. Instead of being aware of his need, the individual reacts defensively to the anticipated shame.

Against that background, a restricted but adaptive self evolves that permits a person to function productively with the assets available to him. This can often be effective, the person gaining self-esteem, albeit tenuous, while cutting off from maturation and self-awareness the selfobject need or needs experienced as shameful. So Mr. Bear built, as he described, an adaptive self—the loner who needs no one and to whom nothing much matters. Problematic, undesirable, counterproductive, and self-destructive as such a restricted self—or "false self," as D. W. Winnicott (1965) called it—might be, nobody becomes a patient as long as

1. Adaptive or Restricted Self
2. Defense against Shame or Guilt
3. Shame or Guilt
4. Unfulfilled, Problematic Selfobject Needs

Conscious | Unconscious

FIGURE 5.1
A Hierarchical Unfolding of Pathology in Therapy

such an adaptation holds up. Seeing the adaptive self for what it is opens the door to acknowledging the existence of the underlying need, and no one will do that unless the alternative is even more threatening and/or painful.

This is, of course, what happened to Mr. Bear. Unhappy as he was, he sought no help until his adaptive self broke down. It is one thing to live as an angry loner, another to incur the socially damaging consequences of publicly threatening to kill. My own belief at this point in the session was that, paradoxically, the need for loving care and attachment is precisely what had made him behave so angrily; through anger his need for help could be signaled without his having to admit it. In any case, what I now wanted to do was not to reassure him that he had not meant to and did not (at least physically) harm his son, but rather to help him see how strong was the defense against recognizing and eventually dealing with the shame that he experienced but so far had not articulated. He acknowledges that he cannot talk about feelings and tries to retreat by mobilizing anger, but it is a feeble attempt and he finds himself increasingly cooperative with me during the interview. His defense against shame does not appear so strong that it precludes therapeutic exploration. This tells me that (1) in all likelihood a formal psychoanalytic approach will not be needed to remove the defense against shame and that a briefer alternative—insight psychotherapy—can be used to give the patient definitive help; and (2) that although he has not yet come to grips with his shame about his need for understanding and help, those needs are close to emerging as he talks about his relationship to his wife, one in which he portrays himself as having to understand her problems.

Toward the end of our interchange, Mr. Bear comes across very differently than he did initially: now a man desperate to communicate and, far from blaming others angrily for his difficulties, he acknowledges that "I'm the problem."

I have gone to some length to trace my thought processes as the dialogue with Mr. Bear proceeded, because it illustrates the back and forth of the therapist's subjective experience and opens the way to a consideration of how one arrives at empathic understanding and guides one's therapeutic activity accordingly.

## Empathic Understanding

Strictly speaking, empathy for a patient's communication involves going beyond only the everyday meaning of a patient's words so as to attend to, and make explicit to oneself, the affective implications of what is being communicated overtly and/or covertly (Basch 1983a). Its usage in our field, however, has made "being empathic" synonymous with "being therapeutic," meaning that the therapist must not only understand the patient's message but must also decide how to use it in the patient's best interest. This necessitates using whatever theory, or theories, about human functioning the therapist espouses to organize what has been heard (Basch 1988).

The therapist implicitly or explicitly thinks, "Given my understanding of human functioning, what the patient is telling me seems to have the following implications for his pathology and/or the healthy aspects of his development." It is then that the therapist is in a position to test the hypothesis by saying one thing rather than another or, for that matter, saying nothing, and then observing the patient's response.

Figure 5.2 outlines the steps involved in this diphasic process. Using this figure as a reference, I would break down my attempt to become empathic with Mr. Bear's first statement in this way: "I had a hell of a time getting here . . . couldn't find a fucking meter." I had the following

I. Steps toward Establishing Empathic Understanding
of a Patient's Communication

   A. Therapist's Affective Resonance and/or Response

   B. Decentering the Therapist's Affective Reaction
to the Patient's Mood

   C. Establishing the Patient's Affective State(s)

II. Steps toward Utilizing the Therapist's Empathic Understanding

   D. Hypothesis Regarding Significance (Meaning)
of Patient's Communication

   E. Therapist's Intervention

FIGURE 5.2
Empathy

affective reaction: I experienced the patient's anger, that is, as it does from infancy on, Mr. Bear's tone, facial expression, and bodily posture generated in me the physiologic experience he was having and that I have learned to identify and call "anger."

I responded first by being taken aback by this unexpected assault; then I felt affronted and momentarily frightened. Was I in physical danger? Would he attack me if he was disappointed?

I found myself taking the next step of decentering (Piaget and Inhelder 1969), that is, stepping back from the patient's effect on me, which required that I separate my potentially distorting affective response from the message the patient was sending. I decided that Mr. Bear really was angry but that my fear was more the result of my own pattern of responding to hostility with exaggerated anxiety. There was nothing so far in his words or demeanor that warranted fear of a physical attack.

I now heard in his anger an aggrieved tone, as if I were to blame for his inability to park easily. There is a big difference between a simple expression of anger, and a display of anger with overtones of blaming that implicitly aims to arouse shame or guilt in the hearer. Stepping back from that message, I rejected it. I could accept his anger but in no way felt blameworthy for his being inconvenienced.

Now that I had dealt with potentially interfering emotional reactions in myself—fear, shame, and guilt—I was able to hear a plaintive note behind Mr. Bear's seething anger. Based on my own past I heard, "Please, Daddy, I need help. But I know I won't get it." There was no way of determining yet whether my judgment here was accurate or whether I was reading something into Mr. Bear's statement. Was I simply identifying with him? That would be the opposite of empathy: instead of experiencing his experience I would just be attributing my own feelings, given the same circumstances, to him. Whether I was being empathic or merely sympathetic would be determined as matters unfolded.

All I could do was ask myself what might be inferred from the patient's anger at this juncture. I switched to step II, D, in figure 5.2, and in anticipation of my responding to the patient's comment, I fit what I had heard and experienced into a theoretical model. Mr. Bear was angry and took an aggressive, hostile posture. What does his reaction say about him?

In our field there are now two differing theories about aggression.

The traditional instinct theory, first formulated by Freud (1923), contends that behavior is governed by two basic instincts that come together in an inevitable, predestined oedipal conflict—namely, the need to discharge sexual tension and the need to discharge aggressive tension. The second theory, to which I subscribe, is based on the research of ethologists, biologists, and neurophysiologists who almost without exception say flatly that aggressivity is not an instinct, that is, something inherently present that must be dealt with but, rather, it is a reaction to frustration (Basch 1975, 1984; Lichtenberg 1989; Rochlin 1982). This view is buttressed by the work of Heinz Kohut (1977), who came to much the same conclusion on the basis of clinical reconstructions in psychoanalysis.

There is no way of responding to a patient without introducing one's theoretical preconceptions, and the content of these assumptions has an overarching effect on the therapy. Two therapists, having heard what Mr. Bear had to say and having come to the same conclusion regarding the affective connotation of his message, would now have their respective responses directed toward different therapeutic goals. The adherent of the instinct theory would think, whether or not the thought was articulated, "Why is this patient displacing his aggression from the oedipal conflict in this manner, and do I think I can help him get back to the true source of that rage, and, if so, how can I best do it?" I organized my thoughts about Mr. Bear's opening statement and its effects on me according to the alternative theory; I regarded Mr. Bear's seemingly exaggerated anger as a response to a significant frustration whose developmental roots needed to be traced. Where the difficulty started, I left open. It might be in any sector of development, including, of course, the psychosexual/ oedipal one.

Having thought through all this, I felt I had become empathic with, that is, understood as thoroughly as I could at that point, Mr. Bear's initial communication, and I said: "Where is your car?"

When Mr. Bear replied, "In the lot across the street," I again went through the preceding process, taking into account not only the content of his statement but the affective connotation with which I perceived he said it. And so it went for the rest of the session. To say one "is empathic," or "is empathic with this or that patient," is presumptuous and inaccurate. At best we achieve an empathic understanding of a patient's communication at a particular time; then we find out if we can do it two seconds later with his or her next statement. Perfection is neither called for nor possible. Much of the time we are at least partially correct about what a patient is consciously and unconsciously conveying to us. But that is enough to do our work; indeed, as Kohut (1971, 1984) pointed out repeatedly, a great deal of our therapeutic work takes place precisely when we find ourselves unable to become empathic with the patient's associations at a given moment. As we learn from patients' words or demeanor that we have failed to understand, and then enlist them in the search for what we need to know to establish that understanding, the patients have a very different experience (a *corrective emotional experience* in the nonpejorative sense of the term) of what is possible for them in human relationships. They may then gradually alter the underlying patterns of expectation that account for their pathology.

We often hear it said that empathy is achieved through intuition, or that the capacity to become empathic, to know what to do, is a gift or a talent—a "gut instinct." What is deceptive is the rapidity with which we may both draw conclusions from what a patient is saying, and then make what we consider an appropriate comment, clarification, or interpretation. When things are going well, our analysis of the situation seems to come from nowhere or, acknowledging the affective basis for empathic understanding, from our gut, that is, from our somatic reaction. However, the speed with which we come to conclusions that permit us to participate with the patient in a back-and-forth conversation, as I did in that initial interview with Mr. Bear, while still considering the many factors that go into a therapist's end of the "conversation," is based on both the rapidity with which the brain processes signals from the patient and transforms these into information, and on the programs a therapist has created for that purpose through didactic learning and clinical experience. Turning the clock back some thirty years, I had the same "guts" then, but often did not have a clue as to what the patient was trying to say to me. There was nothing intuitive about my interchange with Mr. Bear, whether on the mark or not. It was the result of the synthesis of learning from experience with patients and from the guidance provided by the theory of human functioning that I had distilled from teachers, books, and articles.

We need theory on both sides of the equation—initially, at least, to make sense of what a patient is saying, and then to make good use of what he or she has said. The impossibility of understanding anything without a theory, some guiding framework that lets us provisionally organize what would otherwise be only noise (remember those early days when nothing the patient said seemed connected or made sense?) creates a problem for all of us: What if the theory is inadequate or possibly significantly flawed? One can be successful in the first three steps in the search for empathy (figure 5.2) and yet be unable to turn one's affective understanding of the patient to good account. I well remember (Basch 1983b) how it felt when many of my analytic patients and I tried, literally year after year, to move forward only to spin our wheels, as my attempts to fit them into the oedipal schema of understanding pathology failed time and time again, until Kohut's understanding of narcissistic pathology became known to me. With this new organizing framework—again, literally—the patients in question progressed in days further than they ever had in years.

The necessity and benefit of theory granted, the downside is the very trap in which I found myself earlier in my career—namely, finding oneself unwittingly trapped by the limits to one's thinking that any theory inevitably imposes (Goldberg 1990). Since no theory is all-encompassing or perfect, this happens constantly and is the reason that ideally steps A, B, and C of figure 5.2 should always precede steps D and E. First one listens to the content of what the patient is saying and the affect that accompanies or perhaps contradicts the patient's words. Then, and only then, is it time to see if one's framework can organize it.

Can one actually hear the affect first and theorize later? That our understanding of what the patient is saying seems spontaneous, instant, and indivisible comes, as I mentioned, from the speed with which the brain operates. The brain is, however, not merely very fast. Serial thinking, as demonstrated by figure 5.2, is an illusion, for the brain operates in parallel process. Steps A, B, C, D, and E are being performed simultaneously. Once we have committed ourselves to a theoretical framework, even as the affect of the patient registers, its implications are being worked out. By focusing consciously on discursive and affective content, however, we can separate ourselves from the conclusions already reached to gain enough distance to see whether the hypothesized fit between data and theory is really there. We as therapists must keep in mind that our theory can be wrong, and if it is inaccurate, we must acknowledge that and, if possible, modify our theory, adopt another, or devise a new one.

Alternatively, if theoretical modification is not possible, it is necessary to acknowledge that (1) we cannot explain what we have heard; (2) our theory is either inadequate or outright mistaken; and that (3) we have to accept this until something better comes along. It was my inability to look objectively at my guiding theory that trapped me in my work with my analytic patients in pre-Kohut days. I either faulted my level of talent, accused myself of stupidity, or blamed what I considered the patients' obstinacy or lack of capacity for introspection. What did not occur to me was that the theory that had been handed down to me was fatally flawed. Strangely, with patients not in psychoanalysis I had no such difficulty. It was obvious that Freud's drive/defense model had little to do with what was going on with these patients. By following these patients wherever they led, I let myself learn a serviceable ad hoc developmental model that I was to refine later by reading outside my own field about what had been learned concerning human maturation, communication, and brain functioning (Basch 1983b).

# CHAPTER 6

## The Emergent Self in Therapy

As MY PREVIOUS DISCUSSION IMPLIES, maturation involves increasingly sophisticated affect management. It is the degree, quality, and maturational level of the affect invested in our patterns of expectation that give our ideas, intentions, and dispositions their meaning and determine behavior. When affect management breaks down and seems beyond repair, people retreat into anxiety or depression or form symptoms in an attempt to contain the damage to the self system (Basch 1988). I have found that thinking about psychopathology in this way is always helpful, but especially so when a therapist, confronted by a confusing story and a seemingly uncooperative patient, tries to become oriented to what is problematic for the patient and what needs to be done. The following case, presented to me in consultation by an experienced therapist, illustrates how the focus on affect can be used to resolve this not uncommon problem.

### Supervisory Consultation: Linda Mallory

*First Session*

THERAPIST: I've seen this patient for six months, and I still don't have a working relationship with her, so I think it's time to get some consultation.

CONSULTANT: Why don't you tell me what's been going on.

THERAPIST: This is a fifteen-year-old girl, Linda, whom I got when her last therapist retired from practice. He'd seen her for three years. She came because of poor school performance. At first they suspected a learning disability, but the LD consultant gave her a clean bill of health, so they thought it was emotional and sent her for therapy.

CONSULTANT: What happened?

THERAPIST: Nothing much. When I talked to Linda's old therapist, he was confused by the case too. She was good about coming in once a week, they'd talk or play games, but, he said, he never got a real feel for her. Her schoolwork didn't get much better, and the parents complained that as she got older she was becoming more of a discipline problem.

This is not an unusual situation. The therapist is ready and willing to help, but for months, even years, remains baffled by the patient. Nothing seems to be happening, but the patient obviously needs help, and so the therapist continues the sessions. In turn, the patient, in spite of his or her lack of improvement, will keep coming to the sessions, because to some extent the amorphous relationship with the therapist is satisfying an unidentified selfobject need. Unless the nature and form of such a patient's selfobject needs are identified and brought into focus, however, patient and therapist will continue to find themselves in the kind of frustrating therapeutic stalemate being described here.

CONSULTANT: What's the background?

THERAPIST: The father and his present wife came to see me initially and I got a history. Mr. Mallory, the father, divorced Linda's mother when Linda was about one-and-a-half years old; the mother, he said, had run off with another man about five months after Linda was born. At that time, he hired live-in help to take care of her. This arrangement lasted till she was three years old; then he married his present wife.

CONSULTANT: Do you know what sort of help he had for Linda?

THERAPIST: I think it was a succession of housekeepers, not nurse-maids, or anything like that. They cooked for him and took care of the baby, too. None of them lasted more than four to five months. But he sounded as if he was very devoted to her and was very good to her when he was home.

CONSULTANT: What does he do?

THERAPIST: Owns a clothing store. Now he's expanded and is downtown, but when Linda was first born he lived right next to the place and could keep an eye on her during the day.

CONSULTANT: Okay. Go ahead.

THERAPIST: Like I said, the father is a nice man. The stepmother, I think, resents being responsible for her. They don't have any kids themselves, so it's only Linda. Both parents work in the store; they try to arrange it that one of them is always home after school, but sometimes she's alone till after dinner.

CONSULTANT: You mentioned continuing school problems and increasing problems with discipline?

THERAPIST: Both father and stepmother complain that they don't seem to have any control over the patient.

CONSULTANT: What do they mean, "no control"?

THERAPIST: Instead of coming home to do her homework, Linda will go to friends' houses after school and not let them know where she is; she comes home after curfew at night. One time she was out bike riding, got lost, never called, and didn't get back till eleven. Understandably, the parents were very upset. They feel she is not responsible. She will go out with friends, is supposed to be home at a certain time, and then will come home later. Apart from her school difficulties, that's really the main problem.

CONSULTANT: That's the problem the *parents* have with Linda.

THERAPIST: I guess that's right.

CONSULTANT: It's not an unimportant point. Especially with children, there is a tendency to accept the parents' narrative as telling the patient's story. As we well know from couples therapy, however, one partner's narrative as to how the system works or breaks down may bear little resemblance to the other person's view.

Well, anyway, you were talking about their complaints about Linda's friends.

THERAPIST: The parents don't mind her friends, but they want to know where she is and who is with her. According to the parents, these kids have a lot of unsupervised parties, and it worries them.

CONSULTANT: Boys and girls?

THERAPIST: Yes, the parents didn't come right out with it, but it was pretty clear that they worry that Linda is going to get sexually involved.

CONSULTANT: Any evidence for that?

THERAPIST: No, the parents think she hasn't done anything at this point, but the potential troubles them. There is a boyfriend, Bruce, in the picture, but it seems to be an on-again-off-again sort of relationship. I don't know much about that yet.

CONSULTANT: Do her parents think she has a substance abuse problem? Alcohol or other drugs?

THERAPIST: The parents didn't seem to think so, but that worries them too. There's quite a bit of substance abuse by kids at the high school.

CONSULTANT: Anything else?

THERAPIST: That pretty well sums up what I got from the parents.

CONSULTANT: So, just from what her parents have said about her, what are your thoughts about Linda?

THERAPIST: She is behaving very immaturely for a fifteen-year-old. Linda is irresponsible. She goes off and does her own thing with no thought about the consequences of her actions.

CONSULTANT: I agree with you. She does sound quite immature. She's a bad liar; most kids her age know how to con their parents. She doesn't cover her tracks very well . . .

THERAPIST: I think she has a real need to keep her parents involved with her—an inability to separate . . .

CONSULTANT: Well, I don't know about that. You've heard some things from her parents that make you wonder why is a fifteen-year-old acting like a four- or five-year-old? Linda behaves as if she still doesn't know, even after repeated incidents, that her parents are going to be concerned about her whereabouts and that she has to touch base; that she has to reassure them and that, as most adolescents do, she has to win her independence in the context of having to answer to her parents. Most teenagers can figure this out. She apparently can't.

THERAPIST: I agree, but what about the reason for it? The history of abandonment. That's why I formulated it as a separation problem . . . I understand it's purely preliminary . . .

CONSULTANT: I think you are already trying to figure out the unconscious reasons for her behavior. I'm nowhere near thinking about such issues. I would need to know much more about Linda's functioning, especially with you in the therapy, before speculating about the underlying symbolic significance of her behavior and the light it sheds on how and why she became the person that she is. So far what I'm hearing secondhand from the parents is possible evidence for core self problems in the sector of autonomy. Linda's coping skills, the working models she has developed for getting along as an adolescent in today's world, don't seem to be very successful. So let's hear about what happened when you saw Linda.

THERAPIST: She doesn't look fifteen, more like eleven or twelve, but she dresses in a sexually provocative way that's out of keeping with that childlike face and figure.

Linda didn't have any trouble talking when I saw her that first time, six months ago. When I asked her how she felt about coming to me, she said she knew her parents were sending her because of her bad grades, but she said she was coming because she likes having someone to talk to. It doesn't bother her that she's not doing well at school. "Maybe I'm just not smart," is what she says.

When I asked her what she thought her biggest problem was, she teared up and said, "Why my friends don't like me." Sometimes they leave her out of activities, make fun of her, and don't return her telephone calls. I said that her parents had some questions about her going to friends and not letting them know where she is. "I just forget sometimes," she said. I tried to get more information about her relationship with father and stepmother, but I didn't get much.

We've been meeting once a week, and she seems to want to come.

CONSULTANT: But you say you don't feel you have a working relationship with the patient?

THERAPIST: Linda keeps coming for her appointments; I have to assume she's getting something out of it, but I don't know what.

CONSULTANT: How about letting me hear a session; maybe we can figure something out.

THERAPIST: *(Referring to her notes)* Here's one from last month, just before I went on vacation. It's the one that convinced me I'd better talk to someone about the case.

CONSULTANT: Good.

THERAPIST: It was Linda's birthday; she'd shown some interest in baking, and I told her that to celebrate her birthday I'd make a batch of my special chocolate chips for her and give her the recipe. When she came in, I wished her a happy birthday and gave her the cookies. She'd been excited when I suggested it the week before, but now she seemed uninterested and said she'd forgotten all about it until just then.

CONSULTANT: How did you feel then?

THERAPIST: Disappointed, I guess . . . and confused. *(That the therapist is in touch and at ease with her own affective reaction to the patient is an important and positive sign. Our ability to experience and be aware of the affective response a patient generates within us is the basis and sine qua non for establishing an empathic understanding of the patient's communication.)*

CONSULTANT: You wouldn't have forgotten that someone was going to go to some trouble to remember your special day, would you?

THERAPIST: Of course not.

CONSULTANT: Linda's not like you, you see. When you treat her as if she were, what you're trying to do goes right past her. In this case you were trying to reach her through the sense of the subjective self—to be attuned to what, using your own experience, you assumed would be her emotional set. Just as you would want under those circumstances, you figured Linda would wish to have her special day be recognized by people who mean something to her. But instead of some expression of happiness, thanks, or what-have-you, signaling that she is gratified by your thoughtfulness, that it has hit the mark, you get the usual flitting from one subject to another, which probably indicates that the patient is still searching for a way to make contact with you in a way that makes sense to her. So let's hear what else happened in the session.

THERAPIST: Linda asked if her parents had called me—they told her they would after they saw Linda's unsatisfactory school report card. I said that they had phoned and was about to tell her what they said, but Linda didn't wait for me to finish. She told me a dream from the night before . . .

CONSULTANT: She tells you dreams spontaneously, or have you asked for them?

THERAPIST: She usually runs out of things to say, and then I might ask her if she's had any dreams. But this one she brought up spontaneously.

The therapist's asking the patient about her dreams confirmed for me that she is indeed trying to pursue a course of therapy that is psychoanalytically oriented—an attempt to fathom possibly conflicting unconscious goals that are interfering with the patient's conscious intentions. But there is no point in trying to plumb what is unconscious until one establishes what the patient's conscious hopes, fears, and wishes are, and what kind of coping mechanisms she has developed. This determination has as yet not been made in Linda's case, and that is perhaps the main reason that the therapeutic transactions sound so disjointed; the patient and the therapist cannot seem to find each other and establish a rhythm that will let them progress.

CONSULTANT: Okay, what about the dream?
THERAPIST: The dream was about a car accident in which she and her friends were involved. There was a big crash and people were hurt, and she could see bones sticking out of the skin of some of the boys. I asked her how she felt in the dream and she said, "scared," but didn't elaborate when I asked her to tell me more.

Focusing on the emotional tone of the dream, not on its content, was correct technique. But rather than asking the patient to elaborate—something Linda has repeatedly demonstrated she cannot do as yet—it would probably have been more productive if the therapist had been more active, picking up on the scared feeling and the sense of disorganization behind it: "Boy, it sure does sound scary. An accident like that—suddenly everything is out of one's control and terrible things can happen. Dreams often reflect our own feelings or concerns in story form—were you having trouble managing things with your parents, friends, teachers?"

Although the manifest content of the dream seems loaded with symbolism, attesting to sexual issues and the dangers associated with them—boys with bones sticking out but in the context of being seriously injured—this is not something that can profitably be dealt with as long as there is still a lack of rapport between therapist and patient.

THERAPIST: *(Continuing)* I asked her how she was feeling today, and she said that she had a headache but wasn't interested in answering my questions about when the headache started or what might have precipitated it. She did say, however, she felt left out by her friends again. They were acting nice for a while, and then they suddenly didn't seem to want anything to do with her anymore. That reminded Linda that a few days before she had been at a friend's house when she was supposed to be at home eating her dinner. Both her parents were working at the store that evening. She didn't call her parents to let them know where she was, and they were very upset when they tried to check in with her and did not find her at home. I said to Linda that maybe her parents didn't understand how hard it is to eat dinner alone. I then added that maybe her sense of loneliness was heightened by my taking a vacation. Linda said she had thought about that because she would have no one to talk to for those weeks. Before I could respond, Linda started talking about what she and some kids had done the day before. When the session ended, Linda left without visible distress and had to be reminded to take her birthday present with her.

That's it for that session. I've seen her twice since then, that is, after coming back from vacation, but it's no different; she comes in and talks, but it doesn't go anywhere.

CONSULTANT: Right, that's the problem; it's not that what she says is insignificant, it's that it doesn't go anywhere.

THERAPIST: I like Linda, and in her own way I think she likes me—at least she's never made a fuss about coming the way some of the kids do. So, what went wrong?

CONSULTANT: Well, I think you're running into some difficulties because the basic orientation to the patient and to the patient's situation has not yet taken place. With patients who are fairly well organized, we can rely on the patient to state her problem, as far as she understands it, and then put it in the context of the rest of her life. That Linda doesn't do that is already very significant. It makes me think that in addition to lacking effective coping skills, she is having trouble on the level of the emergent or basic sense of self; that is, she doesn't know who she is in relation to others. Just because Linda is young and seems confused doesn't mean, however, that we can use her parents' or any other informants' picture of her as a substitute for Linda's making herself and her situation clear. If the patient can't do it spontaneously, then you as the therapist have to become active in helping her to do so.

THERAPIST: If it's help with basic organizing that Linda needs, what should I do? I tried to set the stage for her when I first saw her and she seemed reasonably at ease with me, but that didn't result in a focus for the treatment.

CONSULTANT: Because then, it seems to me from what you told me, you became so preoccupied with both what you had been told about Linda's history and what the parents had told you about their problems with her now, that you lost sight of what the *patient* was concerned with. I think you were on the right track when, after she told you that she knew her parents were sending her to you for school problems, you asked her what *she* thought her biggest problem was.

THERAPIST: "Why my friends don't like me."

CONSULTANT: Exactly. You were right on the mark with that question, which also conveyed to Linda your readiness to look at her and her situation from her point of view—and she responded. Her distress around her belief that her friends did not like her was accompanied by tears. The appearance of strong affect is paydirt— that's where we should dig. But instead, after getting a little elaboration of that statement, you used it as a lead into the problems her parents had with her not coming home on time or not letting them know her whereabouts; that's when you lost her; her affect disappeared and she just sort of shrugged off their concern.

THERAPIST: So you should focus on and stay with the patient's distress?

CONSULTANT: Not necessarily "distress," but whatever the leading affect might be. If a patient came in, for instance, and said, "I suppose I should talk to you today about another one of those fights I had with my son over the weekend, but to tell you the truth, I'm more interested in a really neat problem my boss assigned me today," I would urge him to tell me about the latter. His distress over the fight with his son is, at least for the moment, displaced by the affect of interest in the challenge at work. That's where the affect is, that's what's engaging the patient, and that's where I can learn what it is possible to learn about that patient at that time. It's the patient's affect that lets you know *where* to intervene, and your assessment of the phase of the patient's developmental functioning tells you *how* to intervene.

THERAPIST: But what about her dynamics—her history?

CONSULTANT: You mean that Linda is a person literally abandoned by her mother at the age of one-and-a-half years, and probably psychologically abandoned by her before that; tended by housekeepers, each of whose brief tenure interfered with attachment and object constancy; now in the care of a stepmother who may resent Linda's emotional needs; and that these circumstances all make her sensitive to separations?

THERAPIST: Yes, that's what I was trying to focus on . . .

CONSULTANT: You may be right about the underlying dynamics, the unconscious motivation for her behavioral decisions, and I would think along those lines too, but the problem is that your attempt to make contact with the patient using that hypothesis has not worked.

THERAPIST: Maybe I'm just too impatient.

CONSULTANT: She's been in treatment since she was eleven or so; did the former therapist have anything to say except what you've told me about the treatment and what had been accomplished?

THERAPIST: No, he couldn't figure her out either. As I said, when she first came to him she was little enough that he tried playing games, checkers and such, but it ended up that's all they did—play games.

CONSULTANT: I'd say three-and-a-half to four years is too long to wait to see if something gels—personally I get uncomfortable if things aren't in some sort of focus by the second or third session, at the latest. Optimally, of course, the kind of organization we're talking about should take place in the initial interview. I am still of the opinion that using your interventions to tap the patient's scripts for dealing with the traumatic separation she has suffered are going to fail. When a patient fears disorientation and disorganization, all her efforts are going to be spent in trying to keep her balance. Look what happened when you attempted to deal with those issues by focusing on the parents' absence at dinner and your impending vacation—she couldn't tolerate it, and you lost her after that.

THERAPIST: You mean I have to approach her on a more primitive, regressed level?

CONSULTANT: I prefer not to look at it that way; regression is not the issue. Once on line, all the domains of the self are functioning simultaneously in everything we do [figures 3.1 and 3.2]. Problems related to orientation are not necessarily more primitive or regressed than problems related to reflection or narration. What I want to find out is whether Linda is doing all she is capable of doing. It's impossible to tell until one gets there what degree of maturation a patient will demonstrate once therapy has really been joined. Once you address Linda's need for defining herself in her present situation as your patient—figuring out what she should or might be doing with you—you may find her functioning at an age-appropriate level, or maybe not. But you won't find out which it is until you respond to her current need, that is, to become oriented. Why not try to follow Linda's affective lead and see what happens? What have you got to lose?

*Second Session*

CONSULTANT: Well, how are things going with Linda?
THERAPIST: I've seen her a few times since you and I met. She talked a little bit about some girlfriends who failed to be sensitive to her.
CONSULTANT: She used the phrase, "failed to be sensitive"?
THERAPIST: She said they ignored her, left her out.
CONSULTANT: How did they leave her out?
THERAPIST: They would get together with each other and not call her; they wouldn't return her calls.
CONSULTANT: What's her explanation for why they leave her out? What might she be doing to create that situation?
THERAPIST: I don't know. I didn't pursue that.
CONSULTANT: I think this is going to be another one of those frustrating sessions for you . . .
THERAPIST: It was. . . . We ended up all over the map after that.
CONSULTANT: The patient is complaining once again about her inability to get what she needs out of her friendships—that was the focus of her affect initially, and it still is. The problem is that, given the opportunity, you don't follow it up, and then you find that she starts wandering all over the place trying to diffuse the affective

103

tension generated within her by having brought up her distress. Your active intervention is needed to give her some degree of comfort with this upsetting material. Unlike a better-structured patient, Linda will not go on to elaborate spontaneously what troubles her; she is waiting for you to help her do that. She is announcing as clearly as she can, "Look, I'm ineffective, helpless in an area that's very important to my self-esteem. Can you fix it?" That's where your focus has to be if you're going to get anywhere.

THERAPIST: What would you have done?

CONSULTANT: Well, as I said, I hear Linda telling me that she is failing interpersonally. The scripts she's written for trying to get along with people aren't working in a situation that is crucial for her. Now, we can't change her situation—we can't change her friends' behaviors or attitudes. If anyone is going to change, it's going to be Linda. Furthermore, right now it's the future we should be concerned with, not the past. We can sit and commiserate with her about how painful it is to be left out; compare those losses with others she's had to endure, and nothing will happen.

This is not a problem that can be solved through affect attunement; there is an issue of competency here. Specifically, it is a core-self problem, a matter of being unable to develop adequate coping skills, not a problem in the domain of the subjective self. We have to get out of the passive voice and into the active one. Not, "What has happened to you, poor dear?" but, "What are you doing to get yourself into this mess?" For example, "It sure is no fun to be left out, is it? It's a real pain. What do you think you're doing that they don't call you?" She might start crying or get indignant. I'd just listen and then might say, "Well, is there anything that has occurred to *you* that you might do differently so they would be more likely to call you?" And you might again get a despairing response to the effect that she's tried this and that and nothing has worked. Then I'd ask, "Whom *do* they call? Who's the most popular girl in this crowd? Tell me about her. What's the difference between you and her? What has she got that you don't?" We have to be careful, however, that the patient does not interpret a challenge to her thinking as a confrontation with her failures and an attempt to shame her. In this sort of situation, I am usually quite explicit in saying to a patient that what I am trying to do is not to make her feel worse about herself, but to help her think about herself differently from her usual way of doing so. It's only by taking a different perspective on the problems that she will be able to see what she can do about her difficulties.

I would not be so much interested in Linda's coming up with either insightful answers to my questions or a program that will improve her relationships with her friends. What interests me is getting her to look with me at the decisions she is making that lead to counterproductive behavior, and inevitably, to a failure of self-esteem. How did she come to those decisions? Nobody behaves in ways that don't make sense; therefore she must have had good reasons, from her point of view, at one time to have written scripts for interpersonal transactions that now are failing to accomplish their goal. Once her present needs are contrasted with past solutions, I anticipate that the patient is, or soon will be, in a different position to make decisions about what is troubling her.

Right from the beginning, using her distress vis-à-vis her friends as a guide, I would have asked Linda again and again in various ways, "How do you look at your inability to maintain friendships on an even keel?" "What have you done about it?" "What have *you* tried to do to make these kids more forthcoming?" For the moment, I connect the patient's dysphoria not with her traumatic past, but with her inability to function effectively. My aim is not to criticize her, but to explore.

At the same time I want to make it clear to the patient that I am interested not in changing her behavior per se, but in helping her to understand that she can analyze her difficulties in terms of her contribution to them. Knowing why and how she sets herself up for disappointment will form the basis for a more effective way of operating in the world and, through that, attaining a better sense of self-esteem. Also, always get examples from the patient illustrating whatever she is talking about. Don't accept vague abstractions; don't assume you understand what the patient is trying to say. Not "Friends," but "Which friend?" Not "They ditched me," but "Exactly what did they do to leave you out?" and so on. The more examples she gives you, the clearer she will become not only to you but to herself, and the more you'll both learn.

## Third Session

THERAPIST: I've got quite a few hours.
CONSULTANT: Okay, let's see how far we get.
THERAPIST: She started off telling me about an aunt, apparently a

young woman, who is coming home from college for the summer. I hadn't heard about this relative before and wanted her to tell me more about her, but Linda said she didn't want to and started talking about her friend Louise instead. Linda is very angry at Louise because Louise will get in a fight with someone, Linda will back up Louise, then Louise turns around and makes friends with that girl again, and Linda feels betrayed. I said to Linda, "Have you tried to talk to Louise about that?"

CONSULTANT: Good. What's she doing about her problems? You are starting to organize Linda actively, giving her some help in going beyond just reciting her thoughts . . .

THERAPIST: Linda got very quiet and started playing with her nails. I said to her that it sounded to me like she was playing hide-and-seek; every time I think we have something to talk about, Linda disappears and I have a hard time finding her again. She laughed and said she knows she does that, but she can't think of what to say next. She then went on to say that another girlfriend, Debbie, gets mad at her and threatens to get off when they're on the phone and she, Linda, suddenly falls silent, which she does often. Debbie says, "Do that again and I'll hang up and you can call me back when you have something to say." I said to Linda that something must be going on that suddenly leaves her tongue-tied; that I would guess there is some feeling that she gets that makes her freeze up.

CONSULTANT: Better and better. Not, "Poor Linda, abandoned once again, this time by your girlfriend," but, "You're undermining yourself as a result of some feeling that takes over at these times." What you're doing is going to pay off.

THERAPIST: She said she freezes up a lot. When she sees her boyfriend, Bruce, unexpectedly in the hall at school he's all smiles, but she often can't even bring herself to say hello. Then he thinks she's ignoring him and gets hurt and mad. She had a big fight with Bruce; he asked her if she had talked to another guy, and she said "No," even though it was a lie, because she was afraid Bruce would be mad at her if she told the truth. I said to her that it sounded as if she was afraid of others' anger. Linda said she's always afraid to say anything that the other person might not want to hear, so she either falls silent or tells lies that she thinks meet the other person's expectations. At that point I heard your voice in my head, "Give me an example, give me an example," so that's what I asked her for . . .

CONSULTANT: You never go wrong doing that . . .

THERAPIST: She said that's how she got in trouble with Bruce and why he is suspicious of her when he thinks she's talked to other fellows while they're supposed to be an exclusive pair. This other fellow asked her for a date and, though she had no intention of going out with him, she said "Maybe," because she couldn't say "No." He told his friends, they told Bruce, and he got mad at her. Then, too embarrassed to explain what happened, she said to Bruce, "It's my business," and compounded her problem.

Then Linda shifted to an upset with her parents. Once again she had not let them know where she was going to be after school, and there was hell to pay when she got home. I said to her that I thought the same thing that was going on with her parents was also happening with her friends; she feels afraid her parents will disapprove of her being away from home and so she can't tell them what they don't want to hear—namely, that she is going to be at this or that person's house in the afternoon. She ends up saying nothing and then she's in deeper trouble when she does get home. Linda said she could see that. I emphasized that the real issue in all these situations was her fear of telling someone something she believed that person did not want to hear, and it was that fear we had to understand better.

CONSULTANT: Excellent. You are now helping her to organize her self by participating in the session, focusing it by exploring what is central for her as indicated by her affective investment. She senses that you are in control of the situation; she doesn't have to worry so much whether she can maintain her sense of self. You are helping to establish a rhythm in the session, and that is not just comforting to her; it gives her the orientation she needs and fosters a sense of an emergent or basic self that she can build on. Like a mother who orients her baby by supplying a background on which the infant can rely in the face of an overwhelming mass of inner and outer stimulation, you are letting Linda know that you are there to receive her messages and can read, understand, and help her with her psychological needs. That's what is letting Linda get organized. Your interventions give her enough respite from the confusing inner turmoil she experiences to become a person in her own right. As a result, she is able to speak more freely and coherently, and you are able to get some real insight into her situation.

THERAPIST: What keeps weaving in and out of the material is Linda's inability to communicate her feelings effectively or accurately. But sometimes I wasn't able to keep the focus on the affect and her problems with it.

CONSULTANT: Who can? No one needs a perfect mother. Not every signal is understood. Not every need is met just so. The important thing is that you now have command of the hours and know what it is you want to do in the context of the patient's material. It doesn't matter if the thread is lost, or seemingly lost, as long as you know what needs to be done and can find your opportunities to get back on track.

THERAPIST: In the next to last sessions I had with her, she was very different. I'd never seen her pleased with herself. She said that she had been able to talk to her parents about going with a group of kids to see some rock concert, and they gave her permission to do so. She said she almost called me first to see what she should say to them, but then figured she could figure it out for herself.

CONSULTANT: Oh, that's great. . . .

THERAPIST: That's what I told her. I said she had made a big step forward, that it probably was not easy to overcome her fear about saying something to her parents that she felt they probably didn't want to hear; but however she did it, she did it, and she must certainly have felt good to see it working out so well.

CONSULTANT: This is really a dramatic demonstration of what I've been trying to tell you—that when we address the patient's issues effectively we see results. As one would predict, once she trusts your ability to help her to define herself—using her affect to help orient her to what's going on with her—she's eager and able to use that productively. You, by responding to her affective signals and transforming what would otherwise be a state of isolation into one of effective communication, have given Linda an experience of safety that she can build on. Now she's moving ahead and developing some workable rules for coping with her life. So, as you can see, once she experienced you in the session in a way that conveyed to her that you understood her need and could meet it, she showed that she is not functioning on a regressed level at all. She has just been waiting for some sense of direction. Has she ever behaved this way before with you?

THERAPIST: Never. She was like a different person. It's a good thing her parents stepped up and played their part. I don't know what would have happened if they hadn't let her go to the concert when she worked up the courage to ask them.

CONSULTANT: It would not have mattered that much. It's good that they were so reasonable, but if they had not been and Linda had been discouraged—"See, what's the good of talking; you don't get anywhere anyway," and so on—you could have said that as far as you were concerned, the important thing that happened was she had the courage to say what she really wanted to, that she has changed, and that you are happy for her and proud of her.

And indeed, she is a different person. She now no longer feels lost and misunderstood. I expected some results when you took hold, but this is beyond my expectations. I mean, she almost called you. What higher compliment could she give you? Essentially she's saying, "I've finally found someone I can count on to understand this huge problem I've got and help me get this monkey off my back." That conviction is so solid that just thinking of calling you was enough to give her the strength to do what needed to be done. Now it's not so much how her parents react that's important to her; it's your understanding and approval that count. By "organizing" her, you have given her a new sense of strength, opened up new possibilities for her—in you she sees an ideal whom she wants to please and from whose approbation she draws strength. It is only once the need for an idealized person is met, and the patient is better able to work out her accommodation to her situation—the core-self issues we were talking about—that the sense of the subjective self can be addressed. That is why now you can validate her effort by praising her achievement and expect that she will be able to respond positively to your validation. What you are seeing is the formation of an idealizing therapeutic transference; she can trust you to support her effectively. It just goes to show you, what we do and how we do it makes a real difference—as long as you were of no use to her she didn't move an inch.

THERAPIST: But she kept coming.

CONSULTANT: Sure. There's something very healthy in this kid; something that knows she needs help and keeps her hoping that maybe next time whatever she needs to have happen will happen—and it did. In terms of developmental theory, she has not given up the hope of fulfilling the basic selfobject needs. Her continued search for friends indicated both her need for and her ability to pursue kinship. Once you met that need by stepping in and orienting her—getting her to make herself clear to you and, in the process, to herself—idealization and mirroring needs fell into place.

THERAPIST: Isn't that awful fast; just a couple of sessions?

CONSULTANT: I've seen this sequence play itself out in a couple of minutes. Once a patient's unconscious needs are responded to appropriately, it's as if the patient says, "Okay, you finally caught on, let's go!"

THERAPIST: Well, I hope I didn't blow it in the last session I had with her . . .

CONSULTANT: You can't "blow it." One swallow doesn't make a summer, but still, what happened and what she achieved is her possession. Even if she were to forget the incident in the sense of not being able to recall it, what she did is in there, and she will never be the same again. But tell me about that most recent session.

THERAPIST: It was strange. She came in saying, "You look like a witch." Then she told me how one of her teachers came up to her and some other kids while they were looking at a bunch of rocks piled on the sidewalk and asked them, in a perfectly friendly tone, what they were doing. And Linda found herself saying, "Maybe we'll throw one of these through your window." She would never do that, and she had no idea why she said it. The teacher got angry at her. Somehow she manages to get all her teachers mad at her, she said, and she seemed to be sad about that.

CONSULTANT: I wonder why she said you looked like a witch? Did you wear a very different style of dress or something?

THERAPIST: No, I was going out that night and had my hair done on my lunch hour. Instead of the way I usually have it, like now, I had it piled on top of my head. I think that's what was different, but I didn't think I looked particularly menacing, like a witch.

CONSULTANT: You didn't look like yourself and it scared her. We've got to remember that not only is she in some respects a very little girl—and babies and even some little kids do have trouble recognizing that the person is the same when some significant aspect of his or her appearance has changed—but also, thanks to your help, she is undergoing some very important changes in her way of looking at and being in the world. When things are changing in such a basic way, a person is more than usually vulnerable to disorganization and anxiety.

THERAPIST: What would you have said?

CONSULTANT: Oh, I think you might have said to Linda, with some humor in your voice, "Do I really look that bad—as ugly as a witch?" The odds are that she would have said something like, "I didn't mean you were ugly," to which I would have added, "Just different." If she agreed, I would have gone on to say, "Linda, I think what's going on is that when you saw me looking different from the way I usually do, you got scared. I think we both know that we're doing some important work together, that what's happening is good, and that you want to keep on going with it. Now when you suddenly see me look different, it's natural to have the thought flash through your mind, without actually knowing you're thinking it: 'If she looks different, what else is different? How dare she not look the way she always does; is her attitude toward me going to change too? Will this different-looking person understand me?' And then, Linda, instead of saying, 'I'm scared—you look different,' because maybe that feels too babyish, you get nervous and say something sort of nasty that you don't really mean." If Linda agreed with that, or even if she didn't, I would have added, "That's what I think happened with the teacher. You are not used to seeing her outside the classroom and she startled you by suddenly coming upon you in the street. Then because, as we are learning, you have somewhere along the line become embarrassed about your feelings and get all tangled up inside wondering what the other person wants to hear from you, out of nervousness you make an uncalled-for comment that you don't really mean."

The important thing for me would have been to show Linda that you are not going to judge her by the lexical meaning of her words but are going to do with her what you hope she can increasingly do for herself; that is, think about the feelings behind the words, especially when these feelings overwhelm her temporarily.

THERAPIST: It sounds right. I wish I had done that, but I didn't.

CONSULTANT: What tack did you take?

THERAPIST: I focused on the affect, at least what I thought was the affect . . .

CONSULTANT: Perfectly fine—when in doubt, explore the patient's affective state.

THERAPIST: I suggested to Linda that behind both her statement to me—"You look like a witch"—and her comment to the teacher—"Maybe we'll throw a rock through your window"—was some anger that we needed to get out and talk about.

CONSULTANT: I think that's right as far as it goes. Anger is, or, I should say, can be the response to helplessness. Linda experienced herself as helpless, overwhelmed by the unfamiliar in both situations, and in both cases made angry statements. So what did she say to that?

THERAPIST: She talked about another situation that had made her angry on the same day that she had that episode with the teacher. She had run for a bus and the driver pulled away without waiting for her. Then she volunteered something interesting. When those kinds of things happen to her, she is able to calm her anger by having fantasies about an imaginary friend who is in the same predicament but does not experience the same frustration: For example, her imaginary friend is very rich, and when she misses a bus or a train simply calls home on her portable phone to have the chauffeur come and get her.

CONSULTANT: Oh, that's very good. She's let you in on her private self—a great compliment to you, and it's something you can use very productively. By focusing on the anger in her statements, you showed her that this is something that doesn't frighten you, that you can talk about such feelings without either condemning her for having them or having to distance yourself from them. As a result she was able to tell you about her fantasy life. That she is able to draw on fantasies to soothe herself is encouraging and surprising to me. I didn't think she had gotten that far.

THERAPIST: But they're such magical solutions—quite primitive.

CONSULTANT: That's all right. Primitive they may be, but the groundwork for that kind of information processing has been laid. You can use this in the future to good account. When she brings up this or that problem, you might ask her, "How would your 'friend' solve this?" If she won't tell you, you can suggest possible ways the 'friend' might take to improve her lot. If she comes up with magical ideas, you can say things like, "Well, if she were only a regular person like we are, what might she do to help herself?" That way Linda will get experience using fantasy not simply to soothe herself but to play out alternatives and imagine the responses of other people to those alternatives, and so on. In other words, she'll feel safe thinking through her actions before jumping in precipitately as she now so often does to escape the pain of uncertainty.

I think you have really turned things around with Linda. Now she experiences you as useful to her. She trusts you to understand her, and that's the indispensable foundation for further work with any patient.

What has happened between Linda and you can be organized according to a schema I developed that divided the psychotherapeutic transaction into six phases: orientation, consternation, reorientation, collaboration, integration, and transformation [Basch 1988]. In the first phase we size up the patient: where does he or she fit in terms of our own past experience? In your case, as is to be expected, you tried to match Linda to the patients with whom you are most familiar—reasonably well functioning people who come in much more ready than Linda was to use a therapist's help. Time after time you found that approach did not work. Now there was consternation: "I don't understand this patient; will I ever?" Then, by following the patient's affective signals and making sure you understood what Linda was trying to say, in other words, looking at the patient's material through her eyes rather than through your expectations of her, you ushered in the phase of reorientation—the appropriate, functional orientation to the patient. Linda responded with collaboration—using your help effectively to strengthen her sense of self and opening the door to further progress. This collaborative effort is what has often been referred to as the "rapport" between therapist and patient.

Linda is no longer just "coming to her sessions": psychotherapy has begun. If this continues, then integration and transformation, using the work you are doing together to create a better-functioning self system, will follow in due time.

# CHAPTER 7

---

## *Restructuring the Self*

---

$B$OB BURDON'S THERAPIST, who had heard me discuss Linda Mallory's case at a conference, called and asked for some supervisory consultation. That was two and a half years ago, so I have been able to follow Bob's progress since that time in semimonthly consultations with her.

## An Extended Supervision: Bob Burdon

*Session 1*

THERAPIST: Mine is a lot like Linda's case. I've treated Bob for over two years, and I just can't seem to get him moving; he's just a blob, just sits there and complains.

CONSULTANT: So, tell me about him—what he looked like when you first met him, what he came for . . .

THERAPIST: Bob is thirty-five years old and single. He was referred to me by Ralph G., a banker from a small town about seventy-five miles away from here, whose wife I treated some time back. Bob inherited a bunch of farms and small businesses when his grandfather died. Mr. G. has been involved in the family finances for years, and he knows the farms and the businesses are doing well, so he was very surprised when, about a year after the grandfather's death, an agent from the Internal Revenue Service contacted him and said they were investigating Bob for tax evasion. Mr. G. looked into the matter and found that Bob had totally neglected to file all sorts of documentation with the government, that his deposits, at least in Mr. G.'s bank, had been way down—all sorts of very peculiar things turned up.

He called Bob to come in for a talk, and, though Bob agreed to get together, he never showed up for the appointments. Finally, Mr. G. went out to Bob's house to meet with him and found things in an unbelievable mess. The house was dirty; Bob, who lives alone, was subsisting on take-out food, or stuff eaten cold out of cans; dirty dishes were all over the place, and, most important to Mr. G., huge piles of unopened letters containing long-overdue bills and forms to be filled out, as well as uncashed checks amounting to tens of thousands of dollars from his tenant farmers and from people who manage the various businesses he owns. Bob had no explanation for his negligence, but was paralyzed with fear.

The Internal Revenue Service people had phoned him also, and he was convinced he would have to go to jail, yet felt helpless to do anything about his financial situation. He knew he should have been more diligent, knew he should have contacted Mr. G., knew he should have retained an accountant and an attorney long ago to help him, but had done nothing. His grandfather had run everything and, after his death, Bob just continued living in the house, taking no responsibility for anything. Paradoxically, Bob is very good with computers and plays all sorts of complex games on the set-up he has in his basement. But he never used them to organize his business matters, something he apparently could have done very easily, given his skill.

CONSULTANT: Where do Bob's parents come in?

THERAPIST: His father divorced his mother and became estranged from the family when the patient was about one year old. He apparently died some years ago; Bob never knew him. He was raised by his mother, actually by his maternal grandparents with whom they lived. His mother seems to have been as incapable of managing her life and its responsibilities as Bob is his. Right now his mother lives in a retirement community in Arizona, supported by a trust fund separate from Bob's holdings, and Bob has very little contact with her. The occasional phone call to her is upsetting and disappointing to him, because she makes it very clear that she cannot tolerate any anxiety on his part and is unwilling to get involved with his life.

CONSULTANT: And his grandmother?

THERAPIST: She apparently was effective, though not particularly warm; she died twenty years ago. I mentioned he never knew his father; also, he never knew the paternal grandparents, or even if they were or are alive.

CONSULTANT: So we have Bob and the mess he's in. I guess Mr. G. took some action?

THERAPIST: Yes, he alerted the lawyer who had managed the grandfather's affairs and they straightened things out. But they told Bob he had to get some help for himself and that's how he got my name.

CONSULTANT: And he didn't protest?

THERAPIST: I think he was just waiting for someone to tell him what to do with his life and terribly grateful that the banker took hold: coming to see me was what Ralph G. wanted him to do and he did it. Actually, once he did come, it was pretty clear that he also knew that he needed help, and he has made no issue about continuing. The problem is that we're not getting anywhere. Now, thanks to Mr. G., Bob's business affairs are being managed properly by people retained for that purpose, but nothing else has changed. He still doesn't take very good care of himself; he exists, and comes to see me twice a week, and that's about all.

CONSULTANT: Well, let's hear what your impressions were when you first saw Bob and what he was able to let you know about himself.

THERAPIST: Since he hadn't been eating properly, I think I expected to see someone in an emaciated condition, but he looks like a big, fat baby. I mean he's huge. He just overflows the chair . . .

CONSULTANT: You said he was a big blob.

THERAPIST: Yes, he's shapeless. There's something so helpless about the way he looks. It's as if his face hasn't been formed by his character yet. Even though he seems very immature, however, there's no question but that he is also intelligent. He pretty much

117

told me what Ralph G. had also said about his situation when he made the referral. He knows what a mess he's in, but he can't do anything about it.

Bob told me that he was continuously depressed and anxious; when Mr. G. rescued him, he was thinking about suicide, though he never got so far as either to plan or implement that idea. He feels his life has just been a long series of failures and of not fitting in. He was a fat, awkward kid whom others picked on. He always wanted to be friends, but nobody wanted him. His mother acted as if he was a chore. If he complained about how he was being treated by the other kids, she would be certain that he was to blame for what happened, but she never told him why she thought so or what he might do to improve his situation. After graduating from high school with good grades, he went to college, but he dropped out shortly after starting—more because he was so lonely than because he couldn't master the material. His only interest since then seems to be reading about and playing with his computers.

He would like to be nice to people and wants to help them, but he found they just take advantage of him because he has money. As a result he has withdrawn more and more into himself.

CONSULTANT: You thought about medicating him?

THERAPIST: Of course, but both his history and the way he interacted with me convinced me that he was *feeling* depressed and *feeling* anxious. He was not clinically depressed; there were no vegetative signs, nor had he ever been truly suicidal.

CONSULTANT: Okay, go ahead.

THERAPIST: After he had told me his history, he said with real distress: "Doctor, when will I be able to clean my house, make some friends, and go back to school?" I guess, from hearing what you said about Linda Mallory, that's where the patient's affect was and that's what I should have pursued?

CONSULTANT: Right.

THERAPIST: I'm still not clear why following the affect is the key.

CONSULTANT: The intensity of the affect tells you what it is a person is experiencing as being most important to him at that time. It's what he is most likely ready to talk about. The distress in Bob's voice as he told you about his inability to function in a reasonably adult manner is the clue that that's what he's ready to deal with in some way. Why change the subject, unless you have a particular reason to do so?

THERAPIST: Actually, I did try to get Bob to talk about that but couldn't get anywhere with it. It's a different situation from the one with Linda. She was all over the place until the therapist got her to talk about her affect; that let her get organized and she felt helped. But Bob was already focused on his inability to function; that's what he talks about all the time, but I can't get further with it.

CONSULTANT: How did you deal with his distress when it first came up?

THERAPIST: I asked him to associate, to tell me more about it. And he does describe in detail what a mess his place is, how he knows he should clean it up, and how he neglected to do any of the book-work for the businesses, and so on. But that doesn't change anything.

CONSULTANT: You said that things got better with Linda when she talked about her affect, but that's not quite what happened. What turned things around was that the *therapist* talked to Linda about her feelings, actively guiding the patient to elaborate the details of what was upsetting her. It was the therapist's properly directed activity that I think reassured Linda that her therapist could be depended upon and could be of use to her. I think you might be running into the same problem with Bob that frustrated Linda's therapist, that is, depending on the patient to set the stage, so to speak. For many patients, our providing a permissive atmosphere is simply not enough; indeed, they often experience the lack of direction as frightening. What happens then is that they either get paralyzed or else spend their time trying to figure out how to please the therapist so that they can get some kind of response.

THERAPIST: How do you know what to say? Some patients respond very well to a listening attitude; Bob doesn't. What's the difference?

CONSULTANT: That's where a model of how the self develops is essential. Anxiety is a sign that a person's capacity to organize and understand what's happening to him is impaired [Basch 1988]. Do you want your patient to be more or less anxious?

THERAPIST: Less anxious, of course. Bob is a bundle of anxiety already, and I want to make it better, not worse. Anyway, why would you ever want to make a patient more anxious?

CONSULTANT: Well, there are well-defended patients, such as the classic psychoneurotics that Freud worked with, and then some of the patients with narcissistic character disorders are highly organized. The only thing that puzzles such patients is why, given their otherwise high level of functioning, they should have whatever symptoms—premature ejaculations with one partner but not with another, a handicapping fear, an inability to enjoy their achievements—are troubling them. These patients have made a virtue out of necessity, defending themselves against their difficulties in ways that are highly adaptive, and often socioeconomically rewarding: the man who defends himself against intimacy by immersing himself totally in work is probably the most common example. Patients such as those need to be made more anxious; by giving them minimal feedback, you create a situation in which the adaptive scripts with which they usually operate no longer work. As Freud found out, what then happens is that the patient, unable to orient himself, regresses—that is, reverts to less mature functioning. In that process the patient, without realizing it, confuses the therapist with figures from his past and transfers to the therapist disappointed hopes, fears, and forbidden wishes that belonged to earlier, problematic times.

As Freud [1915c] taught us, therapeutic reticence creates the necessary therapeutic anxiety to bring about the transference in such patients. All we need to do is instruct the patient to tell us what he is thinking and feeling, without our responding in the conventional way to his questions, comments, and so forth [see also pp. 47–48].

THERAPIST: That's free association. . . .

CONSULTANT: That's the psychoanalytic method. Free association is a misnomer. The whole point that Freud was making is that the patient is not "free" to say anything—that what comes out, if we don't interfere, is not free in the sense of being random but, rather, is *determined* by the patient's unconscious fears and wishes.

THERAPIST: That's how I was taught to treat patients. I never thought of it as anxiety provoking.

CONSULTANT: Sure it is; we've all been in situations where our usual way of dealing with life doesn't work; that's a disorganizing situation. In our attempts to try to get back on track, we often end up saying and/or doing things that we hadn't intended. That's how reporters work. If the person they are interviewing says he has nothing more to say, they don't fill in the gaps with chatter, they just continue to hold a microphone in front of his face. The silence is so uncomfortable for many people that under those circumstances they give away precisely what they had not meant to betray.

But, anyway, to get back to Bob, I would agree with you, he's already very anxious, and there is nothing to be gained for the therapy by making him more so.

THERAPIST: What do you think I should do?

CONSULTANT: Let's look at his self state [figure 3.2]. I think we'd agree that, unlike the psychoneurotic patient, he does not seem to be suffering from a difficulty created by a discrepancy between the domains of the narrative and the private self. That is, his problem is not that there are aspects of the private, symbolic self that are prevented from reaching the domain of the narrative self and consciousness. How about localizing his difficulty in terms of the subjective self? Is he an otherwise well-functioning person who feels alone and not understood, who needs to be reassured that his feelings are not foreign to you but, quite the contrary, evoke an empathic echo?

THERAPIST: I don't think so—he sure isn't a well-functioning person. Bob just keeps asking, "What do I do?" I've told you the state of his affairs—he can't seem to do anything for himself. I think he does feel very much alone, and I do feel sorry for him. I have commented on his lonely, isolated state, but it does not seem to mean much to him.

CONSULTANT: Exactly. This was the initial mistake that Linda Mallory's therapist made. She thought that by conveying her understanding of what she assumed Linda must be feeling, she could be therapeutically effective, but since Linda's most immediate problems were not at the level of the subjective self, that didn't do the trick. The same is true for Bob. Furthermore, as you indicate, he's not operating very well in the domain of the core self either, is he? The rules for managing his life in an age-appropriate and situation-appropriate manner are not in evidence.

THERAPIST: So the focus on Bob's treatment should be on his sense of an emerging self. That's all that's left.

CONSULTANT: I think that's correct. Right now everything is a jumble for him. Since his grandfather died he hasn't been able to organize himself, to orient himself to the ordinary tasks of life, much less to the demands made by the businesses he's inherited. Not that he necessarily has to have the skills to manage all these enterprises, but what strikes me is that he cannot ask for help in getting done what needs to be done. Yet he's been around his grandfather for years and must have been exposed, it seems to me, to enough of grandfather's activities to know whom one calls upon for assistance with such things as income taxes, for example—indeed, he said as much.

What I suspect is that there is a developmental arrest that won't let him use what he has learned until earlier needs are addressed. That's why, when he asked, "What do I do?", I would have said something like, "I think I can appreciate the way you feel, Mr. Burdon. Not to be able to take care of yourself as you expect yourself to do at your age is very distressing. However, what we have to ask ourselves is not, 'What should you do now?' but, rather, 'How did this come about?' But I would not ask what for him would be an anxiety-provoking, open-ended question like, "Tell me about your childhood." I might ask, "What were your experiences as a child when it came to planning your activities?" In that way, we position ourselves to get the information we need while at the same time assisting him in focusing specifically on what we want to find out. Then I'd want to know when, and from whom, he learned how to take care of his things; who took an interest in the friends he had or helped him to deal with difficulties in making friends; who helped him with school assignments and the inevitable anxieties around performance, and so on.

From what you have told me so far about Bob, and from the way he behaves, I would bet that no one ever did take an interest in organizing him and teaching him the necessary skills at various phases of development. If that is true, the affective consequences of being left on his own too soon need to come out in the open. In that way one would be addressing the domain of the emergent self, offering to help him orient himself to his present situation by making it understandable in terms of the past—not telling him what to do and taking over the job—but suggesting implicitly that, with appropriate help, things don't have to remain as they are.

## Session 2

THERAPIST: Nothing has changed. Bob and I are still stuck as before.

CONSULTANT: Okay, let's hear about it.

THERAPIST: I have to admit I didn't do what you suggested.

CONSULTANT: Oh?

THERAPIST: I just don't feel comfortable dealing with a grown-up as if he were a child and I his mother. It's too infantilizing. This patient is immature enough already. If I encourage his regression how will I ever get him out of it?

CONSULTANT: Good question. I should have talked to you about that last time. I never treat a patient as if he were an infant or a little child. What I do do is to talk to the patient about the child within him. I ask him to come over to my side of the room, so to speak, so that together we can look at this little boy who seems to be running his (the grown-up patient's) life.

THERAPIST: If he's indulged enough, there'll be no incentive to ever grow up. Why should he ever give up therapy if he's found the mother he's been looking for?

CONSULTANT: I disagree with your premise. It's people who have had their early developmental needs met in reasonable fashion who can become independent; there is an inherent thrust toward competence that, given a chance, asserts itself [Beebe and Lachmann 1988]. You can't undo the past, but the closest a person can come to healing his self is to understand what has happened to him, and that can only happen in the context of being understood. As you retrace the steps of this patient's development with him, you may indeed be seen for a time as the "understanding mother," and/or "father," and be subject to the demands an infant or small child makes on a parent, but that doesn't call for "indulgence" in the sense of meeting that need as he at that moment wants it met. What we can give a patient—and it is what he *really* needs—is an acceptance of what he's reexperiencing and, sooner or later, help with understanding what that experience meant both in terms of his overall development and the situation in which he finds himself today.

Your fear of infantilizing Bob is, I think, a fear that if he gets in touch with his early needs and the disappointments around them, you won't be able to handle it. Perhaps it is *your* fear that Bob is reacting to in his desperate "But what should I do, Doctor?"; it's a repetition of what went on with his mother, who still makes it clear that she can't tolerate anything but superficial involvement with him.

THERAPIST: That might be right. I'm not familiar with this way of working.

CONSULTANT: That, of course, adds to the anxiety. But that's what I'm here for. I think it's very safe to go ahead with Bob and let him express his needs and then help him deal with them. As I suggested last time, when he brings up the "What should I do, Doctor?", I'd ask him, "Who ever did that, that is, told you what to do and helped you to do it?" "What's the first time that you can remember that someone sat down with you and explained how to go about doing something, or helped you to think through some situation that you were scared about facing?"

Let's try it. If there's anything that comes up that you feel you can't handle and want to talk about before our next appointment, just give me a call.

*Session 3*

THERAPIST: Well, I did it.

CONSULTANT: And?

THERAPIST: Just as you predicted, outside of the school setting, Bob was at a loss to recall any occasion when he had the experience of being guided or helped in achieving some task. He remembers quite clearly how he withdrew from sports because he had no man to teach him the rudiments. His father was of course not there, and his grandfather never had the time or inclination for such activities. Bob didn't want to look stupid in front of the other kids. He always thought of himself as clumsy and, having no family member to practice with him, he didn't want to take a chance and participate in games. He pretended he wasn't interested and became a loner, eventually an outcast.

CONSULTANT: What did you say to all this?

THERAPIST: Mostly I just listened. Once he started to gear up, he hardly stopped for breath. I think I commented on the fact that it must have been very lonely for him, that even now, recalling it, he sounds sad.

CONSULTANT: That's fine; you're focusing him on the affect and, also, letting him know that you hear more than the content of what he is reexperiencing.

THERAPIST: Wait till you hear the fireworks the next time he came in.

CONSULTANT: You're seeing him twice a week?

THERAPIST: Right, it was a couple of days later. He said that he had a terrible dream and thought he'd better leave treatment. Of course, I asked him to tell me what happened. He said he dreamt he woke up from a dream and had "turned into some sort of disgusting creature, something from a horror movie." In the dream, he looked down on himself and saw claws instead of fingers; long, matted hair covered his body; he smelled bad. Terrified, he went to the mirror and it was even worse than he'd thought. But then he looked at his face, and he saw that, looking through his eyes, as if they were window-panes, was a cute little boy, and that was also himself.

He was reminded of a time he had come home crying to his mother—he thinks he must have been about seven years old—because some boys had ganged up on him, beaten him up, and pushed him in the mud. His mother became terribly upset and berated him for having gotten so filthy. She had no compassion for his hurt and acted as if he must have done something to bring this on himself. She behaved as if he owed her an apology. He recalls clearly that at that moment he concluded that he was some kind of freak and deserved whatever was done to him. He made up his mind never again to look to his mother for sympathy—and he hasn't. He was sure that I saw him as his mother did, and that is why he thought that he had better leave therapy.

CONSULTANT: And your response?

THERAPIST: I said I didn't see any freak—I was paying attention to the little boy that he had seen in the dream, a little boy who, I thought, was trying to tell me something, and I wanted to hear it. That relieved him, and he decided maybe he wouldn't have to leave therapy just yet.

CONSULTANT: He was frightened by the longings stirred up in him by your perceptive comment in the previous session, when you commented on his sadness as he recalled having no one to help him learn what he needed in order to keep up with his peers.

THERAPIST: One simple comment brought all this out?

CONSULTANT: It wasn't just your comment as such, but what it signaled to Bob that made the difference; that is, you were no longer afraid of his needs. Just as I told Linda's therapist, I've seen it time and time again, when the patient's unconscious recognizes that you're ready to hear what it has to reveal, it takes off—just as Bob's did with that great dream. And you handled that very well.


## Sessions 4–5

His therapist told me that Bob continued to explore his childhood with appropriate affect. He then began to complain of vague physical symptoms: headaches, upset stomach, and light-headedness were among them. He did not have his own physician, and the therapist gave him the name of an internist he could consult. Bob did so and was given a clean bill of health. Had Bob been my patient, I probably would have done the same thing to reassure both of us; but I think I would also have said that his symptoms seemed to be a reaction to the unsettling effects of his affect-laden exploration of a difficult past.

About three months after I had begun supervisory consultations with her, the therapist reported that the patient came into a session dressed not in his usual slovenly, disorganized fashion, but in a newly bought suit, clean shirt, and tie. Bob told the therapist that he felt good and that she had been very helpful to him. The therapist complimented him on his apparel. She was therefore quite surprised that he came into the next session feeling depressed. She commented on his change of mood, and Bob said that he felt she might be envious of his new clothes and that had spoiled the occasion for him.

I felt the patient's setback was a reaction to the therapist's empathic

126

failure (Kohut 1971). The therapist had focused her praise on the patient's clothes rather than on the achievements that the clothes represented. I would have been inclined to say something on the order of these comments: "You really look great, so well put together. I think your decision to buy and wear these new clothes reflects what's been happening inside of you—getting organized and starting to live up to your potential. And it's nice of you to acknowledge my help; I'm certainly pleased to play a part in what's happening to you." In other words, I'd be validating his sense of a stronger self and, perhaps, offsetting a fear of being shamed, which is often present when someone who has not been responded to in the past now dares to present himself as different from the person he was and, he hopes, more admirable than he had ever thought of himself as being.

THERAPIST: Well, I guess I messed that up, but Bob has continued to come and, as far as I can tell, is making progress in looking at himself and what he's doing. He doesn't look so fancy each time he comes, but he certainly is continuing to dress neatly, much better than before.

CONSULTANT: I'm not surprised. Your ability to accept his needs and your willingness to respond to them appropriately hasn't changed. Therapy, like the rest of life, has its ups and downs, but most patients won't throw in the towel just because something goes wrong once in a while. Basically, he is very content with what's happening, and he should be. My God! If every time we made a mistake the patient left, none of us would be very busy.

THERAPIST: So you make mistakes and have empathic failures too?

CONSULTANT: Of course—can't help that. As Kohut [1971] pointed out, those times when the therapist—recognizing that he has failed the patient—acknowledges this directly or indirectly and is not defensive about his mistake, usually become eye-opening experiences for the patient: a parental figure can admit error and, if possible, correct it. That's usually very different from the way he was dealt with in the past, and expected to be dealt with now.

THERAPIST: If you'd been treating Bob and caught on to his disappointment that you were making a fuss over his clothes and not him, what would you have done?

CONSULTANT: Usually all that's needed is to point out the patient's change in mood and to acknowledge that one may have hurt his feelings by some error of omission or commission. You don't have to fall all over yourself or go to great lengths to "make up" for it—that's disparaging the patient's ability to deal with the real imperfections of any relationship. It's the understanding of and legitimization of his feelings that is important to the patient.

THERAPIST: If I were in Bob's situation and you said that to me, I'd probably say: "Oh, that's okay, I'm thirty-five years old, and it's pretty ridiculous of me to be so upset over such a little thing like that."

CONSULTANT: Then I'd say: "It's true that you're thirty-five years old. But when we lay our self-esteem on the line, when we're looking for emotional affirmation, we're vulnerable to being misunderstood and feeling hurt whether we're five, thirty-five, or sixty-five." Something like that will usually help the patient to see that he should not be so ashamed of his need: that what's really important is not so much the disappointment itself, but the shame at being seen disappointed—seen wanting something. That's what's such a problem for so many of our patients who learn to be ashamed of their emotional needs early in life.

## Sessions 6–16

Bob continued his exploration of the possibilities open to him. He began to attend the Sunday services of the church his family had belonged to when he was growing up. When the minister called for volunteers to help out with the church-sponsored Cub Scout group, Bob offered his services. He was very offended and withdrew from the church when he was questioned closely about his interest in young boys when he himself was not a parent, not even married. This incident, he felt, proved that he was some sort of dangerous freak, and that everyone recognized it. The therapist reminded him of his dream and said that the freak is what his mother saw in him in her anxiety, whereas in reality there was a nice little boy who needed to be understood. And they were able to talk about his interest in boys as representing his wish both to participate vicariously in a childhood he never had and to give to others opportunities for a relationship he would have wanted to have when he was that age. After that session, the patient said that for the first time in his life, he not only began to shower regularly, but enjoyed soaping his body.

CONSULTANT: You were able to turn what could have been a psychological disaster for Bob into a positive experience. As he did when he was a little boy, he came home, so to speak, beaten up; but unlike what he recalled happening back then with his mother, you did not blame him for his unhappiness, did not get anxious about your ability to help him, and were able to show him that you understood him when others apparently did not. You were able, in Kohut's [1971, 1984] terms, to perform a selfobject function: to restore the integrity of his fragile sense of self when it was significantly endangered. In other words, you functioned as an ancillary self, supplying what he needed but could not muster in this case— namely, the confidence that, though hurt and misunderstood, he would survive and go on.

THERAPIST: Yes, he has continued to make progress. He is starting to work more actively, both at home and in his business. He found that there are many things that he can do in the way of repairs around the house—he turns out to be mechanically quite gifted— and he has started to use his computer skills to keep track of his income and his expenses.

CONSULTANT: I suppose his feelings about himself have kept pace?

THERAPIST: Absolutely. His appearance and personal hygiene continue to be much improved, and the way he talks and carries himself is much less babyish.

CONSULTANT: No more whining?

THERAPIST: No, that's true. I hadn't even thought about that. Now, if he presents a situation and asks for my advice, his "Doctor, what do *you* think I should do?" is really a question and a wish to discuss things with me and not a demand that I wave a magic wand.

CONSULTANT: So it seems your fear of some sort of parasitic, infantile attachment if you met his needs was an unfounded one.

THERAPIST: He is progressing, not regressing.

CONSULTANT: Exactly. Depression and apathy represent retreats from making decisions. With your help, that is, letting him use you to strengthen his self, the developmental spiral [figure 1.1] is now on an upward course. You entered the developmental spiral at the level of self-esteem, indicated that you saw him differently from the way his mother had—that his need to be understood was neither shameful nor burdensome. This selfobject experience with you let him begin to make decisions and behave in ways that put him in contact with the world rather than reinforce his isolation. The evidence of his competence continues to increase his self-esteem and so on; you've got the ball rolling.

THERAPIST: He's becoming much more realistic about his mother. She's sick now—developed a fairly serious diabetes late in life—and he calls her dutifully, but he doesn't expect anything from her. He made a tape of one of their phone conversations and played it for me—and it is true—she immediately shrinks from any substantive issues he brings up. As he ruefully said, "Every phone conversation we've ever had she ends by saying, 'Bob, take good care of yourself,' but she's never told me how to do it."

CONSULTANT: At one time mother was all there was, and he had no choice but to turn to her. Now he feels safe depending on you.

## Session 17

The patient continued to function well, gradually extending his activities. He joined a computer club and, through that, signed up for a class that trained him to use advanced software programs for his businesses. He became very admiring of the therapist; he praised her skills and, for the first time, became aware of, and commented favorably on, the decor of her office. In other words, his need for someone to idealize in his life was being met by the therapist, and being cared for by the idealized person permitted Bob to think better of himself and behave accordingly.

He had been driving an old car in bad repair that his grandfather had left him, and he began to think he might want to buy a new model. He thought about buying an expensive import and then became very concerned with the therapist's car: "Do you drive a Cadillac or a Jaguar?" From that he went to wondering in what sort of house the therapist lived and whether she was a millionaire.

THERAPIST: I didn't know what to do with that. I didn't think it was appropriate to discuss the details of my economic life with him, so

I just asked him to tell me what he felt his asking those questions meant.

CONSULTANT: That old chestnut.

THERAPIST: Yeah, it didn't go anywhere. What do you think I should have done?

CONSULTANT: Well, one thing you might have done, since you didn't know what to say, would have been just to have said what was on your mind: "Bob, I don't know what to do with your question. I don't think an answer about my house, my car, or fortune would be helpful, but there must be a reason for your asking. Do you want me to be rich? Or what?"

THERAPIST: What's the difference between your approach and mine?

CONSULTANT: I'm straightforward about not knowing what's going on. To ask, "What does it mean to you?", unless you think the patient is really ready to tell you and just needs a little push, is an evasion of one's puzzlement that doesn't fool any patient. So what if we don't know? The patient may feel he needs an omniscient doctor, but that's a burden I don't want to carry. Besides, the fact of the matter is that when patients have been helped, it has been by fallible therapists like you and me. It's often helpful for the patient to see that the doctor doesn't know and is not afraid to say so. It helps with the patient's shame at not already knowing everything he should to be better.

THERAPIST: So what happens now, do you think?

CONSULTANT: What was his affect when he asked you about your car, house, and finances?

THERAPIST: Very intense—a real pressure of speech—I felt as if he was pushing me into a corner. I guess that's what I could have focused on—the intensity of his affect.

CONSULTANT: Right, and he'll probably come back to it next time.

THERAPIST: Yes, he doesn't let things slide. He usually picks up where he left off.

CONSULTANT: Okay, but if a patient doesn't pick up on previous material and there is some unfinished business you want to talk about, then there is no reason why you can't take an opportunity in the session to say, "You know, there was something last time that I've been thinking about that I'd like to talk about again with you." It often surprises patients that they don't disappear from

131

your thoughts once a session is over; the realization is usually a pleasant revelation.

But, anyway, I think what you're seeing here is the patient's struggle in an idealizing transference [Kohut 1971, 1984]. It seems paradoxical, but really isn't, that as the patient learns to trust you and to feel sufficiently protected by your devotion to his welfare and your capacity to understand him, that he should become frightened about your ability to withstand his needs. What happens is, at first he gains the freedom to trust you, to look up to you, and can let himself be helped by you as you; then, as he gets more secure, he unconsciously reexperiences with you, that is, transfers, the childhood relationship with his mother, and then he gets a bit confused about whether you are the mother he had or the mother he wants. Now he gets scared. Are you going to be as inadequate and threatened by his potential for growth as his mother was? Can he afford to continue trusting you? When he asks whether you have a big car, a big house, and a big fortune, he is asking only whether you are sufficiently "big," that is, secure in yourself to tolerate his ambition, his wish to have a good life of his choosing. Or does he, as with his mother, have to serve your needs or fit in with your programs in order to keep you going?

THERAPIST: Ok, how do I get to that?

CONSULTANT: As we said, through the affect. I'd take it back to childhood: "Bob, behind your questions about my life-style are really strong feelings—I can hear that in the tone and intensity of your voice—this is the sort of thing I don't think you could express in childhood and had to hold back." Let's see what he comes up with.

## Sessions 18–37

The patient was reassured by the therapist's ability not only to tolerate but to welcome his ambition. He continued to toy with the idea of buying a very expensive foreign car, but he decided to rent such an automobile first. He then came in complaining of anxiety; he felt paralyzed and was reluctant to use the car. The therapist explored with Bob whether his excitement about having access to something so luxurious was disorganizing for him. This discussion permitted the patient to function once again. He came to the conclusion that much as he liked this automobile, he also realized that it was not suitable for his purposes and would probably attract negative attention in his community. Eventually, he decided to buy a car that had all the features he wanted but was a more or less standard model. Bob engaged the therapist in a discussion of his purchase and seemed pleased by her interest and response. In the following session he was withdrawn, however. He was suspicious of the therapist and wondered if she, like his mother, was interested in him only because of her needs. The therapist, recalling the incident with his new clothes, realized what had happened, and interpreted to Bob that his dysphoria might very well be related to her focusing with him on the car rather than on what the purchase said about him and his much-improved decision-making process. This interpretation was effective in calming Bob and restoring his good feeling.

In her therapeutic interaction, the therapist was illustrating an ability to turn the inevitable empathic failures that occur in any treatment into selfobject experiences for the patient. She was showing him that, though painful, a misunderstanding of his needs does not mean that he has to retreat defensively; understanding can be restored. Following this incident, the patient demonstrated increased capacity to evaluate his situation, to experiment with solutions for problems, and to modify his approach when indicated—doing for himself very much what the therapist had first done with him. An excellent example of the process that Kohut (1971) called *transmuting internalization* (see also pp. 147–48).

As Bob's sense of core self became firmer, as indicated by his readiness and willingness to engage in various business activities and to take increasing responsibility for his personal life, he reflected that his former low opinion of himself had been unnecessarily harsh. He realized he had all sorts of abilities and dared to be proud of himself. He then asked the therapist whether he could come only once a week rather than twice. Wanting to underscore his progress, the therapist was inclined to agree, but knowing she would have supervisory consultation before Bob's next visit, she postponed coming to a decision about the frequency of appointments.

My impression was that his request to reduce his appointments might very well represent a retreat from the heightened feelings he had for her, as he found himself feeling increasingly positive about, and admiring of, the therapist who had helped him so much. At least, that possibility should be explored.

When the therapist broached the subject with Bob, he immediately associated to the embarrassment he had suffered when he felt like being demonstrative with a teacher who had been kind to him when he was younger. This memory, however, only strengthened his resolve to reduce the frequency of his visits.

In the next session, he experienced fears that the therapist was controlling him. He said that it was now time for him to make his own decisions and that he would come only once a week. The therapist felt that his argument had merit and agreed.

Before his next appointment, Bob called and left a message on the therapist's answering machine to the effect that he felt it was best that he drop out of therapy, and he canceled the upcoming session and all future appointments with her.

The therapist telephoned me to ask whether she should call the patient. I suggested that she not do so. Under the circumstances, I thought, Bob would find what he would interpret as her "pursuit" of him too overstimulating. My impression was that the idealizing positive transference to the therapist was strong enough to bring him back to therapy. I thought that, developmentally speaking, as Bob's sense of core self became increasingly firm, his search for the therapist's explicit affective response (the sense of a subjective self) was bringing him into conflict with the shame such needs evoked early on, when his mother had been unable to deal with such longings. Because of this situation, the therapist was unwittingly placed in a dilemma: not to have acknowledged Bob's progress would have repeated history and injured him further, but the validation that she gave him played into his unconscious fantasies and aroused the shame associated with them. Having resolved this conflict by running from treatment and his longing for merger with the therapist, and having successfully tested his ability to leave her if need be, I thought he could now let himself return.

## Sessions 38–40

Bob called the therapist to say that, after all, he wanted to see her one more time. During that appointment he said that though he found the therapist helpful as a sounding board for everyday experience and was grateful, he had to leave because he felt she was controlling and manipulating his feelings—making him think things that were "bad." With some hesitation he was able to respond to her request for an example: "Sometimes when you put your legs up on the footstool, I want to look at them." The therapist replied that that was something perfectly normal for boys, and as he was reliving so many aspects of his childhood with her, it was not surprising that the curiosity he had then about how women are built also finds itself being repeated in the sessions. The patient, visibly relieved by the therapist's matter-of-fact and nonreproachful tone of voice, came to the conclusion that treatment should continue.

Soon, however, Bob wondered whether the therapist was really saying what she felt or whether she was concealing her contempt for him. The therapist told him that far from contempt, she admired his courage to face openly thoughts and feelings even when they made him feel ashamed. Here I noted the freedom that the therapist now demonstrated in using her own affect and the salutary effect this had on the therapy of this emotionally stunted man.

In a subsequent session, the patient noted that he felt better about his body and was joining a weight-loss program.

Bob recalled how intrusive his mother had been throughout his boyhood until he reached puberty—always checking on his bowel movement and making sure he had wiped himself carefully, insisting on washing or inspecting him at bathtime, but always finding fault with whatever he was doing, and expressing her disgust for his body.

CONSULTANT: You handled these sessions very well, and the patient's responses show that. I think it's especially important that you did not take his sexual curiosity as the sexual interest and intent of an adult or a teenager, nor did you immediately link his curiosity about what's under your skirt to earlier sexual interest in his mother. These things may all be there; we'll have to keep these possibilities in mind, but right now he needs to know that his interest in you and in your body is not overwhelming for you. It's the equanimity, the calm acceptance by the parents that, under healthy circumstances, lets the child traverse the oedipal phase of psychosexual development without necessarily getting tangled up in an oedipal conflict [Kohut 1977]. At this point in the therapy, you correctly addressed the patient in the domain of the emergent self, orienting him to his excitement.

THERAPIST: In his childhood it was all turned around. The mother indicated her uncontrollable interest in his body . . .

CONSULTANT: . . . And then dealt with her uneasiness about that by getting disgusted with the patient and making him feel that *he* was doing something wrong.

THERAPIST: Wait till you hear this . . .

CONSULTANT: Okay.

THERAPIST: Bob became very excited about some innovations he had introduced into his computer on the basis of the course he was taking. I was caught up in both his enthusiasm and his interesting way of presenting what he was doing. He is actually a good teacher, making what might otherwise be a pretty dry subject come alive. In the next session, Bob was again quite excited. After he left me, he realized he felt very good because I had sat forward in my chair and my face showed real interest in what he was saying. "You were excited with me, and it wasn't sexual," he said. Whenever he got excited as a kid, his mother would get disgusted with him and turn away.

CONSULTANT: Not too long ago he could not tolerate his excitement; now he can take pleasure in it because you respond to it appropriately and in kind. Your affect attunement, a form of "mirroring" as Kohut [1971] calls it, addresses the sense of subjective self; Bob has come a long way with you.

THERAPIST: You're excited too.

CONSULTANT: Of course, it is exciting to see this happen.

THERAPIST: I feel good about your excitement the way Bob felt about mine. So you are mirroring me.

CONSULTANT: Yes, I don't really like the term *mirroring* very much because it sounds a little phony, a bit patronizing, at least as far as I'm concerned. When I say, "mirroring," I'm thinking "validation." For me the important thing is that your attempts at validating the patient's experience take different forms, which depend on the particular domain of the self that you're addressing. Affect attunement is only one form of validation, or mirroring—very appropriate when the patient is in the domain of the subjective self, as Bob was here—but it isn't applicable across the board. When we recognize the patient's need to be oriented, or comment on and help the patient with the need to develop appropriate ways of coping with whatever he's facing, that, too, is validation, or mirroring.

Anyway, closer to home, my obvious interest, pleasure, and excitement in what's happening addresses the sector of the subjective self in your professional identity and validates your work and your right to feel good about what you're doing. And, of course, as your consultant, I also feel validated by what's going on between you and Bob. We are all individuals, but we three also form a system, and our developmental spirals overlap. Bob's increased self-esteem affects all of us in a positive way.

## Sessions 41–42

The patient reported that he had been thinking about himself as a happy baby who had the therapist for a mother; then he would think of his real mother and imagine that, with her, he must have been just a miserable lump of flesh. He asked the therapist if he might tape some sessions. He needs, he said, to have more opportunity to think about what's going on between them.

THERAPIST: I did give him permission to do so. Was I wrong?

CONSULTANT: You have doubts?

THERAPIST: It felt okay in some ways, but what if he treats the tape like a fetish, a disguised form of sexual gratification?

CONSULTANT: Well, other things being equal, I always prefer errors of commission to errors of omission. If the taping was the wrong thing to allow, its effects will show up in the patient's behavior, his affect, and his associations, and then you can deal with those issues just as you have with other aspects of treatment that didn't quite work out. You talk about the effect of what happened and acknowledge any part you played in that situation. So you're not perfect— we've gone through that with Bob—and I would expect that, just as before, properly handled, an error in technique gets turned into a therapeutic benefit for the patient.

I think you have better reasons, however, for letting him go ahead and tape the sessions than just "feeling it was okay in some way." Here you've taken Bob, who was disoriented, disconnected, and disorganized, through the orienting experiences that led to his forming a sense of emergent self; you helped him come to a much healthier adaptation to his circumstances than he had ever had before. In this way, you strengthened the sense of a core self and found that he was responding in the domain of the subjective self to your affectively attuned response to his excitement about his increased competence. I would think that his wish to tape his sessions with you is in the interest of developing and strengthening the domain of the sense of a private self. He's already told you that he can now juggle you and his mother in fantasy; play with the idea of what it would have been like if things had been different. So I think you were quite right to let him go ahead and tape the sessions. He does not sound as if he is preoccupied with you as an object for sexual desires. The issue is attachment and how safe it is for him to express those needs.

THERAPIST: It seems to be working out; there were no untoward repercussions from the taping. At first he said that he liked to hear my voice but was disgusted by his own: he heard not himself as he imagined himself now, but a frightened patient who is fearful of doing something wrong. But he persisted, nevertheless, in recording another session and then came in saying, "We really sound good," replaying for me the parts that he felt were especially outstanding. He didn't just focus on the tapes, however; along with this he was doing all sorts of things, including now taking an active part in his various enterprises and their financial management. He explains what he is doing very proudly, and clearly enjoys my positive response. So we keep working in the domain of the subjective self right along with the strengthening of the private self.

CONSULTANT: Yes—and the domain of the emergent and core self too. Once the pathway is opened up, all of them get worked on simultaneously. You can't be strengthening the sense of a subjective self without influencing the other aspects of self organization that have been freed up.

THERAPIST: Bob told me that what I tell him truly makes sense, but it helps him only because now he can really hear what I say and think about it.

CONSULTANT: Bob is developing good insight. What he's talking about is a function of the private self: the ability to objectify events and then think about them.

THERAPIST: Bob soon stopped taping our sessions. He said he found himself remembering and thinking about what we talked about without referring to the tape, so he didn't have to do that any more.

## Session 43

Bob was becoming somewhat expansive as he continued to find himself able to think and perform in ways that he never suspected could be his. His mother had convinced him that he was a very limited individual, whose tendency toward excitement was dangerous. That none of this was true felt heady indeed. He compared himself to the mythical Phoenix; he would rise from his ashes and become admired where he had been despised. The therapist's voice, as she told me this, carried an uncharacteristic sarcastic overtone, inviting me to laugh with her at poor Bob's pretensions.

CONSULTANT: Does Bob's expansiveness embarrass you?

THERAPIST: Yes, I think it does.

CONSULTANT: The Germans have a saying that love for the self stinks; it is usually said to children when they are full of themselves so as to deflate them.

THERAPIST: Bob is so, so, immodest . . .

CONSULTANT: The monster or freak his mother was so afraid of—who turns out to be a little boy thrilled with his ability to function in new and, to him, surprising ways. Think of him as Big Bob and Little Bob simultaneously. At the same time that he is going into his adult role, he is also making up for lost time in childhood, going through some of the developmental stages that he never had a chance to traverse back then.

Try not to identify with Bob and confuse your embarrassment and your memories of trying to show off and making a fool of yourself in the process—and we all have those stored up—with his still unashamed, boyish exuberance, which is very healthy. We

139

don't want to bring him down because of our embarrassment, as parents often do with deflating comments ostensibly meant to prevent children from getting too swell-headed. Instead, let's take credit for making this possible for him.

THERAPIST: What do you think I should do or say?

CONSULTANT: Listen to him. Control your inward squirming by thinking about development and where this kind of behavior fits. Once you're able to use the theory to decenter and separate your feelings from his, you can become empathic with his communication [figure 5.2]; your consternation will dissipate, you'll get reoriented, and then once again be in a collaborative effort with Bob.

### Session 44

As I should have been able to predict, Bob's grandiosity did not last too long. Some of his great plans for himself were frustrated by circumstances, leading him to become very unhappy with himself: he would never amount to anything, and so on. I suggested to the therapist that it might be well to introduce the patient to the concept of the developmental spiral, which will help him understand that the all-or-nothing way of looking at oneself is a remnant from childhood and that the world doesn't run that way. Competence and self-esteem are achieved incrementally. Between the decision making and the achievement of competence, there are usually a lot of back and forths, trial and error, until the right combination is achieved. Very important—it is not just the end result but the way in which one tries to get there that adds up to competence and healthy self-esteem.

### Session 45

Bob came in very concerned about what he called his selfishness. He finds himself fuming inwardly when service in a restaurant is poor, getting irritable, and taking it personally when other cars on the road don't follow the rules properly—in other words, he wants things to go his way. The therapist said to Bob that she was not put off by what he called his selfishness. As he himself noted, perhaps he was not as tolerant an adult as he wanted to be, but this so-called self-centeredness was a normal part of childhood experience that he only now permitted himself to have. He was catching up, so to speak, on attitudes and feelings he could not afford as a kid, when he had to be abnormally self-effacing. "Actually it's good," she said, "that these feelings are coming out now; you're not acting on them and don't have to be so hard on yourself for thinking about them." The patient replied: "You're not my mother; she would have said, 'You're awful.' "

When Bob again began to dwell on his disappointment that he was not able to succeed at everything he had set out to do, the therapist explained the developmental spiral to him. Subsequently, Bob found himself very productive. He took his computers out of the basement and installed them in a room that had a view and lots of sunlight: this he designated his office.

He found himself increasingly angry at his mother for what she had done to him but concluded that she had no choice to be other than she was. Looking at himself, he realized that he, too, would have remained emotionally handicapped, leading an unnecessarily limited life if it had not been for his therapy.

Returning to his former analogy, he said that, in terms of the developmental spiral, he could be that phoenix, arising not from ashes, but from decisions he could now make that would free him. "Maybe," he said, "I can't be a doctor like you or have a family, but I can do other things that people can look up to."

I was impressed by the therapist's relaxed and self-possessed tone as she talked about these sessions. There was no trace of the defensive sarcasm previously evident. As I have noted repeatedly in myself, our own characterological difficulties tend to recede in therapeutic encounters once we understand how to handle them with the patient. It is quite likely that in then helping the patient, we also end up healing ourselves to some extent.

## Sessions 46–47

THERAPIST: Bob continues to be very excited that I taught him about the developmental spiral. Now he wants me to teach him more.

CONSULTANT: It mobilizes and reinforces the kinship transference, Bob's previously thwarted need to be accepted as one of the group.

By teaching him something about the tools you use, you brought him into our guild. That means a lot to him.

THERAPIST: Yes, when he was talking about this, he got quite disturbed when he thought about his grandfather's never teaching him how the business worked or preparing him to take over some day.

CONSULTANT: Apart from the very real problems that this created when grandfather died, it was a psychological exclusion: you are not one of us.

THERAPIST: No one seemed to appreciate his amazing capacity to deal with computers.

CONSULTANT: That's right. That lack of recognition undercut the development of autonomy in Bob. We've been focusing on attachment issues, but now that that aspect of his life is being handled so much better, autonomy issues—the freedom to function as a center of initiative, as Kohut [1971] called it—will be coming to the fore.

## Sessions 48–49

Bob, in the middle of telling the therapist something, stopped and said, "You look like my mother. Your face is blank." The therapist realized that family concerns of her own were indeed interfering with her ability to react with interest to what Bob was saying. She acknowledged as much and was able to involve herself wholeheartedly in the remainder of the session. Bob returned next time very animated. Again he called attention to the difference between the therapist and his mother, "You listened to me and cared enough to straighten yourself out."

THERAPIST: It was during that session that I realized why Bob always reminds me of a baby. He scans my face continuously and will not look anywhere else.

CONSULTANT: Yes, I think he's affectively lost much of the time, though getting a lot better. As Tiffany Field's [1985] experiments have shown, the mother's facial expression calls forth in the baby's face the same expression, which is accompanied by bodily sensations associated with that particular affect—joy, anger, interest, and so on [Basch 1976, 1988]. In this way the baby experiences and "knows" what mother is feeling. Tracking mother's facial expression is an important part of both self and mutual regulation. Bob is not a normal baby insofar as he can't take his eyes off your face. Normal babies scan the mother's face and, once satisfied, look elsewhere, then go back to mother's face, and so on [Beebe and Stern 1977; Beebe and Sloate 1982]. Bob is a desperate baby, searching and searching your face to make sure he understands the message or, perhaps, that he'll find what he needs there. That he hasn't given up, however, that he's still looking, is a very good sign.

## Session 50

Bob, rather shamefacedly, told the therapist that he is often overwhelmed by the emotional content of a TV program or by the lyrics of a song on the radio. He finds himself crying or getting excited, pacing up and down, waving his arms in the air, and often gets so wound up that he can't go to sleep at night. The therapist explained to him something of the nature of affect and its development, and pointed out that his mother's inability to tolerate affective expression impaired what would have been the normal progress of his affective development. Now he is in a better position to experience affect and channel it into feelings and emotions, but the process takes time. It is understandable that he is at first temporarily overwhelmed by the basic affective experiences that he can now permit himself. Bob became pensive; then his face lit up and he said, "Doctor, I never realized that what's happening here (pointing to his head) has anything to do with (the sensation) here (pointing to his chest and abdomen)." Following this session, the patient found himself much better able to keep his house in order and, for the first time in years, cleaned up his yard.

Bob's readiness to deal with his affect and the therapist's assistance in helping him to gain intellectual control over what was happening to him affectively permitted a large maturational step in his cognitive/affective development. Now, instead of struggling to suppress his affective reactions lest he be overwhelmed by them, the patient welcomed these experiences. Affects had become feelings and, therefore, could now serve as informative messages that helped maintain the self rather than threaten its stability. As is usually seen under these circumstances, the patient's maturational steps forward in one sector of development have a ripple effect: In fixing up his house and yard, Bob let the environment reflect his enhanced scope of self, whereas before it had portrayed his forlorn state and low opinion of his functioning.

The patient did not volunteer, and the therapist did not inquire into, the nature of any fantasies aroused by the TV programs or the music Bob had mentioned. What would I have done? I think I might have asked the patient about this, but certainly would not have pushed for such information. Even had fantasies emerged, I would have filed them away in memory for later reference. At the time I would have pursued the course chosen by the therapist: exploring the patient's formerly arrested affective development and the shocking, paradoxical effect of finding himself confronted with the discomfort that progress in the psychological sphere often entails.

## Session 51

Bob continued to feel very good about himself. He told the therapist about his diet and his progress in losing some excess weight. He got excited telling her how, in his effort to fix up his house and yard, he had devised an idea for special shelves to hold his tools and was in the process of building them.

CONSULTANT: Again, something we might have expected. When a patient no longer needs to flee from his or her affect, the liberating effect often spills over into the developmental sector of creativity, and the patient can then give free play to all sorts of talents. Creativity is too often equated with originality. Very few of us have the capacity to make a truly original contribution to culture, but, psychologically speaking, Bob's figuring out how to build a shelf that suits his purposes is just as creative as some genius coming up with an answer that changes the way we live or think.

THERAPIST: Bob was very excited about what he was telling me, and I, of course, let him see that I was excited for him. But he didn't remain happy for long. His thoughts turned to the way his offer to help with the Boy Scouts at church was suspiciously questioned; then he thought about some similar situations when his motives were misunderstood as a child and wondered if maybe he basically is a "monster." I told him that he came in proud and excited to our session and that he had every right and reason to be so. His thoughts of being a monster, I felt, had to do with his mother's inability to share his excitement and her making him feel that there was something terribly wrong with him for feeling that way. That seemed to make sense to him. Then there was a new development.

The next time he came in, he was carrying some psychology self-help books. He told me how much he was learning about himself from them, implying that this was much better than anything we had done together. Most of what he told me was pretty self-evident stuff, but I heard him out and did not criticize him or the books. A lot of what he said he learned from them were issues we had discussed and resolved, but again, I did not comment on that.

CONSULTANT: That's painful, isn't it? It feels like a slap in the face— deflating, humiliating. Paradoxically, however, it is precisely your success as a therapist that has necessitated Bob's retreat. I think he had to dilute the excitement he experienced when you, very appropriately, got excited with his progress. He wants and needs that, but at the same time it's so new and different from what he's experienced that he had to back off. Looking to these books was his way of doing that.

*Sessions 52–53*

Bob continued to read and rely on pop-psychology books and downplayed what he and the therapist were doing. He concluded that he needed a man's opinion and thought of contacting the author of a particular self-help book that had impressed him.

THERAPIST: When I saw he was serious, I said that if he wanted a consultation with a male therapist, I would help him with that. That served to satisfy him for the moment. I think I was handling his depreciation of me and our work pretty well, but then he started accusing me of cheating him, taking his money under false pretenses. That's when I lost it and told him that, if he believed that, we were finished.

CONSULTANT: I think I missed the boat the last few times. I've been explaining his reactions exclusively as a dramatic contrast between your ability to tolerate his excitement and to be proud of him for his progress and the situation with his mother, which was certainly quite the opposite. But I think what's also going on is that Bob is now behaving like an early adolescent who needs his freedom, but acts as if it can be achieved only by angrily rupturing the parental bond that he has counted on for so long. He's trying every which way to fight with you and, as these kids always do, finds your Achilles' heel and gives it a good swift kick. You can't help but feel, "How could you, after all I've done and tried to do?" He may have to leave you for a while, but maybe he can learn that he doesn't have to do it in anger.

THERAPIST: It's already happened. When I confronted him, he became frightened; he seemed taken aback that I was angry—couldn't believe it—but I assured him that I really was; this was no pretend game. He apologized indirectly, saying that we know how manipulative his mother had been and that's how he saw me at that moment. I told him that was something we could talk about.

In the next session he commented that I looked different. We agreed that it wasn't my looks, but the previous emotional exchange that made things seem so different. At the same time he continued to report progress in his daily life and his feeling about himself. His excitement about his accomplishments doesn't seem so bad to him any more. I again explained that his mother's not only lacking an affirmative response to his excitement, but being positively afraid of it had made him feel there was something dangerous about that state. He then recalled how, on one occasion, he had been the only one able to figure out why the fish were dying in an aquarium in one of his science classes, and that the teacher had been very excited and praised him in front of the class. At that time he recalls having experienced an unaccustomed glow of pride.

Bob then suggested that since he was now doing well, he needed to see me only periodically if problems arose. I said that we should continue monitoring what was going on with him on a regular basis, and that perhaps a fear of my not being able to tolerate his progress was making him back away. He agreed to continue, at least for a while, but he found reason to cancel the next two appointments and just left messages on the answering machine that he would not be in.

CONSULTANT: Well, we'll see. Your deeply felt anger when he hurt you may have led to his realization that he no longer is a child: he is now really an individual with responsibilities not only to himself but also toward others. He may have to struggle alone with his psychological adolescence.

## Session 54

THERAPIST: Well, I didn't see Bob. He wrote me a letter in which he thanked me for my help but also told me that he would not be coming in any more. He felt that he knew enough about himself to continue growing on his own. He said that now, when he ran into problems, he would think of calling me, but then he would "be my own psychiatrist," reflecting on what was bothering him and the reason for it, and then come up with his own solution.

CONSULTANT: How do you feel about this turn of events?

THERAPIST: I am pleased, but also disappointed. I worry about how well he will get along. I wish he had given us a chance to work through the termination.

CONSULTANT: Me too. It's certainly also happened in my practice. This unilateral breaking of a bond that we as therapists aren't prepared to relinquish just yet is a shock every time it happens. There is that momentary shame—a sort of a role reversal—when I'm confronted with my dependence on the relationship with a patient. But that's okay. There should be an emotional investment; you nevertheless think of what you might have done or should have said that would have made for a different ending. In other words, the way Bob ended makes us feel incompetent; our self-esteem is at risk, and we start thinking of ourselves instead of Bob and his situation. Once we put things in perspective, however, that he not only feels a need to be on his own but finds himself thinking of you and then doing for himself what the two of you would have done together in the past, is actually the desired result. Again, it sounds as if there has been a transformation, a further transmuting internalization: that is, your way of thinking about problem solving has increasingly become adapted to his particular needs. That he had to leave abruptly is probably the equivalent of the adolescent rebellion that I mentioned before. Adolescents are unable to express their sadness and affection when they leave: "I don't want you or need you any more" is the best they can do. That usually is related to the unresolved sexual issues. Bob probably has to run away now not only because he needs to try his wings, but also because he became more aware of you as a woman and can't handle that yet.

THERAPIST: So there's more to be done.

CONSULTANT: Yes, but just as adolescents leave home and continue their maturation on the job or in the college environment, so may Bob now have a chance to work out some things for himself. He may feel the need for more professional help and either come back to you, or, as is often the case, find someone else to pick up where the two of you left off. It can happen that returning to you would be experienced as a return to his former self. He may need another therapist both to help him move on and to resolve issues raised for him in your relationship. You were, after all, the first psychological mother he had. I think you should be very pleased with yourself once you disabuse yourself of the notion that we all seem to have, namely, that if we really knew what we were doing, our patients would be forever trouble-free and perfect when they leave therapy. Bob has really come a long way, thanks to you. From next to total helplessness to a hopeful, if still shaky, independence, is quite an achievement.

Bob, in paying his last bill to the therapist, left one session unpaid for. The therapist sent a bill for that visit a month later, but no check was forthcoming. I suggested to her that the patient, needing to maintain contact with her, would use the monthly reminder in that fashion, and I suggested that she stop billing him. Three and a half months later, the patient called for an appointment and came in. He said that his primary reason for consulting the therapist at this time was to talk to her about a problem he was having with one of his employees and whether he could trust the individual in question. He described the circumstances and the therapist discussed the situation with him.

As far as he was concerned, Bob said, he was managing his businesses and his personal life with increasing success. Indeed, the therapist noted that he looked well and that he was appropriately dressed, quite cheerful, and energetic. There was something "appealing" about him that had not been in evidence before.

During the interview he mentioned that he had once again been contacted by the Internal Revenue Service regarding a supposed irregularity in his return. This time, he noted, he did not panic, but instead contacted his legal adviser, who was only too happy to take charge of the situation and relieve him of any anxieties around it.

As the therapist's consultant, I could not have been more pleased with what happened. I was glad that Bob benefited as much as he did, but, at least when dealing with a graduate therapist, the patient remains the therapist's and not the supervisor's responsibility. The supervision is of the therapist, not of the patient. It is the growth of the therapist, not the patient's improvement, that gauges the efficacy of the supervisory process. It was gratifying to see how, as she learned to understand and use the developmental model, the therapist was freed to use her total personality not only with Bob, but with other patients she discussed with me. And, as the patient grew in response to her increasingly confident and affectively responsive leadership in the therapeutic sessions, the therapist's enhanced competence and attendant sense of self-esteem not only altered the conduct of her practice, but, from what she told me, positively influenced other aspects of her life.

Supervision is not psychotherapy, and one must be careful to remain on the proper side of the line that divides the two: That is, attempted interpretations of the therapist's intrapsychic life and its influence on the treatment should be strictly avoided. A comment such as, "You are acting out your unconscious aggression on the patient," is an improper and unwarranted assumption. Only the therapist's therapist would be in a position to make such a statement.

On the other hand, psychotherapy is not a substitute for supervision, an exercise in teaching the application of theory to therapeutic technique. Both personal therapy and supervision can and should have a salutary influence on the therapist's professional and personal development. In terms of the therapist's developmental spiral, her exposure to the developmental model gave her a theoretical framework that let her make those decisions about her therapeutic interventions that led to competence. The resultant enhancement of self-esteem, as indicated by her confidence in using the full affective scope of her personality not only with her patients but in her interactions with me, attested to her achievement.

We have long known that unexamined and misunderstood personal problems hinder the therapist's effectiveness with his or her patients; it is often not recognized that a theory too limited to let the therapist understand and respond appropriately to a patient's need is just as much of a handicap. Too often an impasse in therapy is blamed on the therapist's supposedly unanalyzed personal problems, when it is the theory that is at fault.

## Postscript

Four weeks after his returning for a consultation, and about four months after he had interrupted therapy, Bob called for another appointment. "This time I'm back for myself," he announced, "not for my business." He thanked the therapist for what she had enabled him to do and reviewed his development as he understood it. He once again contrasted the therapist with his mother: "Mother gave birth to me, but she could not raise me; she never played with me; she never smiled at me with her eyes, like you do. But there was no one else, and I clung to her. I thought she was perfect and that I had to be perfect. Now I can manage my life and my business and deal with problems without everything having to be one hundred percent."

He said that he was continuing to do well, but there is a nagging anxiety that something will happen to destroy him and all he has accomplished. He feels lonely. He realizes that he has difficulty with intimacy, especially with women. Here the therapist commented, "That's probably why you had to leave me." Further associations led the patient to iterate that he felt his mother was uncomfortable with his maleness; it would have been easier for her if he had been a girl. They agreed to resume therapy once a week.

After several weeks, Bob confided to the therapist that he was attracted to Belle, a young woman who worked in one of his stores. Belle responded in a friendly manner to his attempt to make conversation; he nevertheless felt ridiculous and was certain he would be rejected if he went beyond superficial chitchat. "I know *you* like me," he said to the therapist, "but I'm a mess."

In the next session he reported a dream in which the therapist demanded sex from him. In the dream, this made the patient very angry and he left the house and cleaned up the yard instead. This led to associations about his mother and her probable misunderstanding of his need to be admired and validated as being sexual.

A week later he hesitatingly showed the therapist a picture of Belle. He had been very excited telling the therapist about her, and both hopeful and worried as to what the therapist might think of Belle. He tried to make it very clear, however, that he was not in love. "Oh yes you are," the therapist told him, "and you feel wonderful being able to feel that." Bob began to cry. He started reproaching himself for his feelings and thinking sarcastic thoughts about himself. The therapist suggested that he was doing to himself what his mother in her anxiety would have done to him under these circumstances.

From what Bob said, it seemed that Belle might be interested in establishing a more personal relationship with him. The therapist helped Bob think through the possible next moves he might make. Bob was very worried; though he was now dieting seriously, for the first time he realized in a different way how overweight he was. His shame prevented him from actually asking for a date at the moment, but he knew he would do so in the near future. "Even if I get hurt, it's worth it," he said, and added, "Even if it's not Belle, I know it can be somebody else, someday."

I thought the therapist did an excellent job, emphasizing the liberating effect of Bob's being able to feel attracted and excited, while letting the external reality unfold as it might. This turn of events also brings home the fact that a focused approach to psychotherapy—one that aims to deal with the developmental issue at hand rather than to let, as does formal psychoanalysis, developmental issues unfold gradually in all their complexity—does not short-circuit or preclude other aspects of development from emerging in due time. Though issues of attachment and then autonomy occupied most of the time in Bob's therapy up to this point, psychosexual material appeared and could be dealt with productively when he was ready to do so.

Under the pressure of his infatuation, Bob continued his program of self-improvement. He continued to shed excess weight, got medical permission to enter an exercise program, which he pursued religiously, and became even more careful of his manner of dress and personal hygiene. It now became clear, however, that his choice of a girlfriend had not been the happiest one. He was awkward in his attempts to get closer to her, and Belle ridiculed his attempts at intimacy while trying to take advantage of his money and position as the owner of the business that employed her.

Within a short time, though she never permitted so much as a hug or a kiss, she got him to buy her clothes, jewelry (fairly inexpensive), and some household appliances as the price for her company. Bob rationalized Belle's behavior as being the result of her deprived upbringing. Just as he had been emotionally deprived, she had been materially short-changed, and for some months he was content to indulge her, hoping that his generosity would touch her and let them become more intimate.

The therapist, correctly I believe, made no attempt to dissuade Bob from continuing his quest. She focused on his feelings and let him share with her his new-found freedom, however awkward, to make a sexually directed attachment. The reality was that the money he was spending in no way threatened his economic well-being. What he was going through in his late thirties paralleled the situation of the class bookworm who, in the throes of the sexual awakening of puberty, spends his earnings from a newspaper route trying to impress the beauty of the eighth grade. We knew that he was going to get hurt but also that we neither could nor should attempt to intervene and try to spare him.

The therapist focused on the intrapsychic significance of Bob's experience: the importance of his attempt to form the attachment, the improvement in his self concept that permitted him to make this move, and the support needed to help him accept the understandable awkwardness and miscalculations that traditionally accompany the first attempts to move into the arena of male/female relationships.

During this time, in addition to the obvious improvement in his external appearance, Bob reported that for the first time masturbation was accompanied by sexual fantasies. Until now, he had periodically relieved prostatic discomfort mechanically and as a matter of routine, thinking of it in the same vein as the need to empty bowel or bladder. Now he began to take pleasure in his sexual functioning.

Several months after he had begun going out with Belle, he made a more determined effort to add physical closeness to their companionship. As she fended him off, he saw on her face the same expression of disgust that his mother showed whenever he tried to get physically close to her. He cried very hard when he told this to the therapist, who reported the incident to me in a tone charged with the hurt and indignation she experienced when she heard it. I felt it too: here was our Bob, whom we had come to know as a kind, gentle, and decent fellow, being treated so callously.

Her spontaneous reaction, the therapist said somewhat hesitantly, was to put her hand on Bob's and say simply, "You are not disgusting." The therapist was very concerned that I would look askance at her making physical contact with a psychotherapy patient. "Oh, crap!" I said, by which I meant, "You did exactly what you should have done." Her gesture gave a meaning to words that would otherwise have been hollow. This was not a countertransference manifestation, that is, an expression of the therapist's unconscious conflict imposed on the patient's transference. The therapist was aware of her emotions and was perfectly correct in extending herself to Bob. In the context of what was known about the patient's personality and problems, and about the course of the therapy, there was little danger that her intervention would register consciously or unconsciously as a sexual overture, which is the bugaboo. In any case, had such a misunderstanding occurred as evidenced by the patient's associations and behavior, then one would deal with it, as one always should, through exploration and interpretation. I have never subscribed to the notion that a kindness shown to a patient automatically commits the therapist to more of the same. Bob's therapist's gentle touch no more commits her to hugs and kisses than my lending a few dollars to a patient who has had his wallet stolen on the way to the office then commits me to lending him money to buy a new car when the occasion arises.

Soon afterward, Bob was able to extricate himself from the failed relationship with Belle. He recognized it as an aspect of his postponed adolescence and was not angry at either Belle or himself for its failure. In retrospect, he recognized that not only their age difference, but the discrepancy in their values precluded any other outcome. He continued on his path of self-improvement and now, much less shy, sought out dates with women whose age, background, and goals were more similar to his.

Therapy continues and, though one cannot predict the future, what has occurred so far gives me every reason to think that the outcome will be a good one.

# CHAPTER 8

---

## *Brief Psychotherapy*

---

$A$ FEW YEARS AGO I reviewed with my students the criteria for patients who are candidates for various forms of short-term therapy (Burke, White, and Havens 1979; Flegenheimer 1982; Gustafson 1984; Strupp 1980a, 1980b, 1980c). The patient who is said to benefit readily from such treatment is one who has suffered a circumscribed, recent emotional trauma, has an otherwise well-functioning character structure, and is prepared to accept the therapist's help—in other words, the ideal patient we all pray for but seldom see. Such patients need only an opportunity to reinforce their mature kinship selfobject needs in order to recover their composure and resume functioning. Their own inner resources are more than sufficient to deal with the problem that confronts, or has been visited upon, them. With such patients all of us can be miracle workers; here, in my opinion, it does not much matter what particular theoretical orientation a therapist subscribes to; the therapist's interest and willingness to hear the patient out suffices to restore quickly his or her emotional balance. The situations I have found instructive are the ones in which patients I considered far from "ideal" or "easy" nevertheless accomplished in a much shorter time than I anticipated what they needed to do to regain competence and restore self-esteem.

## A Struggle for Independence: Marcus Lavelle

Mr. Marcus Lavelle, a thirty-five-year-old astronomer, came for psychiatric consultation on the recommendation of his section chief. He was neatly dressed, look much younger than his stated age, and spoke with a high voice in a somewhat stilted manner.

MR. LAVELLE: Now that I am here, I am somewhat at a loss as to where to begin.

THERAPIST: Why not tell me what brought you here.

MR. LAVELLE: All right. I have seen myself become increasingly upset lately, and my work at the observatory has suffered noticeably. My immediate superior had occasion to question my performance when I made some unpardonable, amateurish mistakes in interpreting certain photographs. I confided my emotional difficulties to him and he, apparently having heard of you, suggested that I seek your counsel.

THERAPIST: And you are upset because of . . . ?

MR. LAVELLE: Oh, just some family arguments. I take them too seriously, get all wrought up, then cannot sleep very well, which leads me to be irritable and nervous, and then I cannot concentrate properly on my job. I suppose I should be able to leave my problems at home and not let them affect my work, but I cannot seem to do that. That my accustomed routine has been disrupted in the last few months has not helped either; I am a creature of habit and do not tolerate change very well. Much as I dislike taking medication, do you think that perhaps I should have some sleeping pills and tranquilizers to tide me over until I can settle down and get back to myself?

THERAPIST: Maybe, but I can't be sure about that yet on the basis of what I have heard from you so far.

MR. LAVELLE: What more do you need to know? I'll tell you whatever I am able to.

THERAPIST: You mentioned that your routine had been disrupted. What patterns does your life take ordinarily? *(Here I attempt to establish a base line for what the patient considers his optimal, or at least customary, manner of functioning. This will then provide a way of evaluating the nature and the extent of the present stress with which he is trying to cope.)*

MR. LAVELLE: Disrupted is an understatement! I had a perfect arrangement. I was subletting from a widow who had built a nice little apartment in the back of her house. It was walking distance from the observatory—perfect for me since I do not drive. She was gone most of the day; it was quiet, and so I could sleep. Much of my work is at night, of course, and over the years I have gotten used to sleeping in the morning, getting up around one or two in the afternoon, cooking something for myself, and doing whatever I had to before going to work. By the time she came back from her job, I was about ready to go to mine, so we never interfered with one another.

Then the neighborhood looked as if it was starting to deteriorate, and her married son urged her to sell the house while she still could get a reasonable price and move to the suburbs with them. In meeting his filial duty, he—inadvertently I am sure—created problems for me. Nothing else even halfway suitable was available nearby and, in any case, the neighborhood was decaying precipitously, so I returned to my parents' home. I suppose they mean well, and I should be grateful that they will have me, but it is driving me crazy to be there.

Not crazy, really, that is not a good word to use with a psychiatrist; that is to say, I don't hear voices or anything like that; they . . . it just makes me very nervous. *(Stops and looks flustered.)*

THERAPIST: Of course, I understand what you mean. Why don't you just go on and tell me about it.

MR. LAVELLE: I startled myself. I became so intent on what I was saying that I forgot where I was. I mean, I have thought about this so often that I must have carried this conversation on in my head a million times, but maybe this is not what you want to hear.

THERAPIST: No, no, you're doing fine. If you weren't, I'd stop you. So just go ahead. *(Apart from the facts about his life that the patient has conveyed, how he has spoken confirms that he has a capacity for introspection. That he interrupts his own narrative at this point and needs repeated encouragement to go on may well indicate that he is coming to some sensitive issue that he is hesitant to speak about. The form that this hesitation takes, however, a recognition of my presence and his wish to meet my requirements, reflects at least adequate capacity for interpersonal relationships. This, and his ability to introspect affectively, tend to offset my fleeting thought that his seemingly isolated life-style might be indicative of schizophrenic or schizoid pathology.)*

MR. LAVELLE: My parents are really very decent people, but, in my opinion, they have never been able to understand me or my interests. Even as a child, mathematics fascinated me, and I preferred to stay in the house and work out problems, or read, rather than going out and playing. My father would try to get me interested in sports and was very upset that I had no desire to play baseball or football, or, for that matter, to watch the television broadcasts of professional or collegiate sports. I think he gave up on me when I was in high school and discovered astronomy.

Actually, my interest in the stars was awakened some years before that. My mother got the idea that it would be good for me to join the Boy Scouts. She, too, used to worry about my being a loner and thought that an organized after-school activity would enforce contact with other boys and lead to my making friends. She was right about that, I must say. I soon found several other boys who, like myself, were unathletic, bookworms, and totally uninterested in and inept at the various outdoor activities so zealously pursued by the other boys and the adult group leaders. *(Pauses and smiles to himself.)* I still remember the seven-mile hike we were required to take for promotion from tenderfoot to second-class Scout. The four of us rode a bus to the meeting point. *(We both laugh.)*

But one of the merit badges that did attract my attention and whose requirements I fulfilled willingly was the one on astronomy. I had never looked at the stars before with anything more than passing interest, but now I became curious and excited as I traced the various constellations. Perhaps I already sensed the mathematical possibilities in the regularity of the heavens. All I know is that I went far beyond meeting the requirements and impressed the merit-badge counselor with my preparation and obvious interest. He had a telescope on his roof and offered to teach me more about the subject. I worked with him all through high school, even learned how to grind lenses, and ended up building my own instrument. *(This is indicative of the patient's capacity to meet kinship, idealizing, and validating needs when an appropriate opportunity presents itself.)*

My parents were pretty upset of course that their son had found something else that separated him from his peers. Between mathematics and astronomy I had no time for anything else. Also, I took a job on weekends and after school to help me pay for my equipment and my books.

If it had not been for my parents' nagging, those would have been happy years. They never could understand why I preferred to be at the planetarium in the company of people, most of whom were much older than I, rather than joining a high-school fraternity and driving around town on Saturday night with the stereo going full blast. I used to try to explain to them what I was doing, but they never understood. I really believe that, to this day, my parents do not differentiate between astronomy and astrology. They were very disappointed that I persisted in my interest when it came time to go to college, and that I did not use my mathematical ability to get a business degree or become an accountant like my father. But there was really not much they could do. I won scholarships and worked, and I did not have to ask them for any help to speak of.

Once in college, I did meet more young people who thought as I did and I felt less like an oddball, but it did not change my existence dramatically by any stretch of the imagination. I formed no great friendships, though when we have occasion to see each other at national meetings and the like, I get along well with people I met during those years.

It is my work that absorbs me and that is why I am so disturbed now. There has never been a time that I could not concentrate on what I had to do. No matter how upset I was, I could always calm myself down by thinking about whatever task occupied me at the moment. You enter a different time frame, you know, and whatever is troubling you does not seem quite so important when you begin to think in terms of light-years. Now I find myself thinking of what is going on at home all the time. I cannot seem to forget about it.

THERAPIST: What is going on at home that you find upsetting?

MR. LAVELLE: The nagging and, behind it, the lack of respect for what I am doing. They treat me as if I still had not made up my mind

159

what it is that I want to do with my life. They behave as if some day I will wake up, stop my nonsense, and get a real job. It is true I do not make a great deal of money now and probably never will, but I will not need that much anyway.

THERAPIST: From what you tell me, your parents' attitude is nothing new. Why would it upset you so now?

MR. LAVELLE: For one thing, I have not experienced it in such concentrated doses for quite some time. It is one thing to go home once or twice a month, quite another to have to listen to them day after day.

Also, you have no idea what it means to me not to have peace and quiet when I need it. My mother has just flatly said that if I do not keep normal hours that is my problem and not hers. I think she goes out of her way to make disturbances when I am trying to sleep. For instance, just a few days ago I woke up to find her rummaging in the storage closet in my room for some blankets she will not need for months.

THERAPIST: Anything else happening to upset you?

MR. LAVELLE: Well, I know it bothers me that they are putting pressure on me to get married so they can have grandchildren. They seem to think that if I only got a real job—by which they mean go back to school, become a CPA, and go into my father's firm— then I would be able to afford to settle down and have a family, like, as they say, normal people.

My parents seem to feel that because I am an only child I owe them this. As they get older, they have become preoccupied with the idea that I am obligated to perpetuate their name and carry on the family firm. To me, this is both ridiculous and outrageous. I resent their questioning me about my relationships with women, their crude attempts to match me with this or that unmarried daughter of friends or friends of friends, their incredulous look when I try to explain to them that I am simply not interested in women. I never have been particularly excited by the opposite sex and I may not be in the future.

*(In a more excited voice)* I serve a function, I am productive, I am, or at least was, reasonably happy and content. Don't I have a right to exist as I see fit without having my own parents look at me as if there is something drastically wrong with me for living as I do?

THERAPIST: The tension in your voice just now . . . it sounds to me as if *you* are doubting that—that you have a right to lead your life as you see fit. Maybe you need their approval?

MR. LAVELLE: Not when I am not continuously in their presence. I feel accepted by my peers; they find me worthwhile.

THERAPIST: That is very important. We don't live in a vacuum. Who we are is, at least to some extent, defined by the subculture in which we function. *(I seem to have decided to work with Mr. Lavelle on the interface of the verbal and narrative sense of self. In other words, I am focusing on bringing his private self into the narrative domain, anticipating that that process will lead him to an understanding that will permit him to make the decisions that will improve his situation.)*

MR. LAVELLE: I still go to work every day and interact with the same people. Why does that not offset my parents' misapprehension of who I am?

THERAPIST: Parents have a direct line to the child within us. They were there long before you were on your own. The doubts about yourself that were laid down by them don't just disappear.

MR. LAVELLE: Are you saying that what I have accomplished is a sham—counts for nothing—that basically I am still the peculiar, not-quite-accepted child my parents saw?

THERAPIST: I think that is exactly what you are afraid of.

MR. LAVELLE: But I am not that child. I found what I wanted to do. I was the one who worked with Dr. Woodbine [his mentor on the Astronomy Merit Badge]. I got the scholarships, and over my parents' objections became what I am. I am who I became.

THERAPIST: Not quite. As you told me, you are now making mistakes at work that you would not expect yourself to make ordinarily. Your section chief doesn't "recognize" you any more, so to say. This is not surprising. When a person's well-deserved confidence in himself is shaken, he may very well find himself relatively nonfunctional. If you no longer believe in yourself . . .

MR. LAVELLE: That's it exactly. I no longer believe in myself. But I do not know why that should be. My degree is hanging on the wall; my publications have not disappeared.

THERAPIST: You behave as if your parents have a point—as if in spite of everything you have accomplished, you deserve to be depreciated.

MR. LAVELLE: I just wish they would let me be.

THERAPIST: They probably can't. In my experience, parents' anxiety that their child cannot survive, much less prosper, unless he conforms to the pattern that worked for them, leads to the kind of nagging that you are experiencing.

MR. LAVELLE: *(With a rueful laugh)* So, you are telling me I cannot even blame them for my misery.

THERAPIST: I'm not taking your parents' side against you. What you experience in their household is real and very difficult for you. But now what? They want you to change and you want them to change. Each party says if the other would only be different, then everything would be all right.

MR. LAVELLE: I see no reason to change my way of life.

THERAPIST: I don't either.

MR. LAVELLE: Do you have a family?

THERAPIST: Yes, I do.

MR. LAVELLE: Children?

THERAPIST: Yes.

MR. LAVELLE: I just do not see myself in that situation.

THERAPIST: You've explained that to me. And why should you?

MR. LAVELLE: You do not think that abnormal?

THERAPIST: No, but I wonder if you do?

MR. LAVELLE: Around my parents I doubt myself.

THERAPIST: That's why they can make you so irritable and anxious. If you were sure of yourself, I don't think they could upset you so. I think what we have to establish is whether you are really comfortable with yourself and your life-style, or whether at a deeper level you are struggling, for example, with sexual feelings but rationalizing them away.

MR. LAVELLE: I have asked myself that.

THERAPIST: And your answer?

MR. LAVELLE: I do not believe that I am just fooling myself or evading the issue. My interests do not go in that direction. There is no struggle around the subject.

THERAPIST: So, then the issue is more your wish for your parents' approval for who you are. It hurts not to have it.

MR. LAVELLE: It really does.

In this first session, Mr. Lavelle showed that he could both articulate his problem and have an appropriate range of affect. In his daily life, he seems to have found the level of attachment comfortable for him. The psychosexual sphere posed no immediate difficulty. His creativity is his strong point. It was in the area of autonomy, functioning as a center of initiative, that I saw the problem. He had dealt with the dilemma of needing his parents' approval to feel whole and worthwhile—and, given their agenda for him, the impossibility of receiving it—by distancing himself geographically and compensating quite successfully for its absence through relationships with others. Now this adaptation was no longer feasible. He was exposed daily to their attacks on his sense of competence. I began in the first session to bring out the problem of his shaky self-esteem, so that we could deal openly with what he had been trying to handle indirectly by removing himself from the stressful interactions of the parental home.

In the second session, a week later, the patient reported that though the stresses at home had not abated, his work was essentially back to normal. He was productive and effective. This told me that his idealizing need to feel appropriately supported at a time of stress was being met by the opportunity to discuss his issues with me. Mr. Lavelle had thought about our session and now elaborated on his loss of self-confidence and self-esteem under both the explicit and implied criticism of his parents. I noted that he spent less time inveighing against their small-mindedness and emphasized more the effect on him.

A new element came into the session when he talked of his feelings for his former landlady. Though they might exchange only a few sentences in any given week, he realized he missed the atmosphere of his former residence. We concluded that what was so important there was that this person accepted him and his way of life: in her house there was not the constant tension of feeling that he was a disappointment and a problem. He missed what she had provided. Should he, dare he, call her at her son's home and see how she was doing? I said that I thought it was a perfectly fine idea, but that I suspected after years of feeling different and unaccepted, a certain amount of shame had built up in him—a readiness to be found wanting, which led him to withdraw defensively from putting himself forward and chancing rejection. Mr. Lavelle was pleased that I had put into words what he felt was indeed the situation. What he would actually do we left up in the air.

In the third session, Mr. Lavelle reported that he had made the phone call to his former landlady and had received a very positive response. She had invited him to have supper with herself, her son, and his family on the coming weekend. Momentarily, her offer put him into a quandary. They lived in the suburbs, and he not only had no automobile, he had never learned to drive. In the split second after the invitation was given, he pictured himself being driven to his destination by his father—like a little boy being delivered to a birthday party and then being picked up a few hours later. He was saved from his embarrassment when his hostess, who of course knew that he had no car, suggested that she would pick him up at the local train station.

His visit, which took place the weekend before he saw me for his fourth session, was very successful. He had realized for the first time that his former landlady regarded him not just as a boarder but as a friend. She recounted for her family how kind and helpful he had been to her during the years of his tenancy: shoveling snow in the winter, helping her unload her car if he happened to be there when she came home from grocery shopping, and so on. He had forgotten all this and had never thought for a minute that these things were noticed or mattered to her.

I said that who we believe we are is influenced by how others regard us, and that the problem was not that his parents were criticizing him, but that he himself had adopted and accepted their view of him, in spite of his protestations to the contrary. He did not see the person that his landlady saw—the respectable young man she was glad to have around. He said that he had come to pretty much the same conclusion. He was very pleased that someone who had come to know him, at least superficially, found him acceptable. To which I added, not just acceptable, but pleasant, helpful, and worthwhile.

He had made, he said, some decisions after analyzing his situation. He had concluded that he was not the problem, nor did he any longer blame his parents for being what they were. The problem was the combination of his parents and himself—like two chemicals, each one stable alone but that when mixed create an explosion. He now felt, he said, that he was indeed the person he had become. He realized that he also had the obligation, like every other adult, to see to it that his view of himself prevailed—that when push came to shove, he could stand on his own two feet. Why should he have to go back to his parents' home just because he lost his residence? He had inadvertently, he said, continued to live as if he were a college student—living away, but home was still Mom and Dad's house. His visit to his former landlady had shown him how helpless he is in a society that depends on the automobile. He credited me with being the stabilizing force that permitted him to come to these insights, but had decided, especially given his limited funds, that what he really needed now were driving lessons. He had already made a phone call to his job-connected credit union to see if, using his modest savings as a down payment, he could arrange for a car loan once he was licensed to drive.

What had happened, I thought, was that, on the one hand, I met his idealizing need and, just as he suspected, served to stabilize him. On the other, it might well be that his dependence on and longing for me became overstimulating—that is, awakened unmanageable, perhaps even homoerotic needs for the father who had not been able to relate to him. In any case, he was dealing with his situation effectively. He had sought out a benign maternal figure and used her to rework his self-image, actively combating the perception of himself as seen through his parents' eyes. He apparently recognized that no one could give him his independence, that apportioning blame for his difficulties was not a solution; rather that it was he who had to make the move to liberate himself in a very practical way. Accordingly, I validated his reasoning and his decision: what he was planning made good sense to me, and I said that I was here if he saw the need for further work in the future.

We parted on this note, and I heard nothing from Mr. Lavelle for about ten years. He then called and asked for an appointment. When we met, he told me that he had married some years ago and now wanted to consult me about therapy for his stepdaughter.

After he ended his sessions with me, he carried out his plan to make himself independently mobile. He made a living arrangement similar to the one he had had before. On the recommendation of his former landlady, he rented a coach house that had become available in her new neighborhood. Not unimportantly, this permitted him to establish a pattern of visiting her two or three times a year, usually around the holidays. Emboldened by his previous experience, he dared to become friendly with the couple then renting to him. It turned out that the husband was suffering from a chronic, ultimately fatal illness. A few years after his death, he and the widow, a few years older than Mr. Lavelle, were married. He reported that they were happy together and that she seemed comfortable with his life-style. Her youngest daughter had complained of emotional problems, and he thought that perhaps some psychotherapeutic intervention was indicated. I agreed and gave him the name of a therapist for her. He thanked me and left, and I have not heard from him since.

Time-limited therapy is not an acceptable alternative for those patients who require the painstaking exploration and reconstruction that only long-term therapy can accomplish. On the other hand, neither is more always better. There are many patients who, when helped to focus on their difficulty, can make excellent progress in just a few sessions and gain the necessary support and insights to carry on successfully without feeling the need for further professional help. In this case I had no idea, of course, that the patient would take the initiative and conclude his therapy so quickly. In retrospect, however, I wonder if he was not right to do so. Patients often sense the limits of what it is they can safely accomplish, and he certainly made the most of our work together.

The next patient to be discussed reflects the not uncommon, and more difficult, situation in which time limitations are placed on the therapy from the outset.

## Big Problem/Little Time: Renée Lobach

Ms. Lobach, twenty-three years old, was a member of the armed forces, who had been sent to a local university for course work, preparatory to undertaking a special overseas assignment that she very much wanted.

Her chief complaint was that she had become increasingly anxious and unproductive. Her final examinations were to be held in six weeks, when she was to be transferred to her new post. However, she knew that if she did not succeed in making a good record, she would be returned to her former duty station and to a job she did not find stimulating.

I asked Ms. Lobach to describe her symptoms more specifically. She said she has had bad dreams and wakes up feeling exhausted. She stays in bed long past the time she should get up, and when she does rise, it may take her several hours to get dressed. She cannot decide what to wear. When she does try to study, she has a hard time concentrating. She has not been particularly happy in Chicago, but since she found her course work relatively easy, her dysphoria did not interfere with her doing well in her classes. In the last few weeks this changed; though she knows she could do the work and get good grades, she cannot bring herself to put in the minimum required to accomplish that.

Here I was faced with the serious problem of a nonfunctioning patient, whose situation was complicated by the brief time available to help her. I now had to decide whether to work within the limitations imposed or refuse to treat her.

Ms. Lobach looked most unattractive. Her face was slightly deformed and expressed contempt. She was dressed, as are many young college students, in jeans, wool shirt, and running shoes without socks, but her clothes looked dirty and were ripped here and there. I thought she looked like a walking insult to the standards of the community. Her manner of speaking only added to this unfavorable impression. Although obviously intelligent, and with a very good vocabulary, she spoke with a perpetual sneer as she downgraded the school, her professors, and her fellow students. Yet, in spite of her inability to function and the impression she made on me, her attitude conveyed that she thought of herself as a very special, desirable person. What struck me was that, though nonfunctioning, Ms. Lobach was apparently not aware of any loss of self-esteem.

Rather than rejecting my negative affective reaction to her or taking myself to task for not liking this human being, as previously discussed and outlined in figure 5.2, I strove for an empathic position by first identifying and accepting my negative response, then stepping back from it *(decentering)* through my recognition that I would always have such a reaction to this sort of appearance, and then realizing that I had to make an effort not to take the manner in which Ms. Lobach presented herself at face value. In other words, I could not be sure at this point whether Ms. Lobach was trying to upset my sensibilities, or whether my prejudices were getting in the way. I was now in a position to see if in time and with further knowledge of the situation I could come to decode the nature of the message that she was trying to send to the world through her demeanor and appearance.

She volunteered that she knew exactly what was wrong with her: her parents were messed-up people who had messed up her life. It always seemed to her that her father had no respect for her mother, but to the world they present the picture of a loving couple. She hated and despised what she experienced as their hypocrisy. She feels that her mother made, and makes, inordinate demands on her for affection and support. Father is emotionally reticent and ill at ease with the patient, but ever since she was a small child, he has tried to ally himself with her by telling her that he and she, unlike her mother, are intelligent and sophisticated; together they can talk about things that her mother would never understand. Somewhat less bitter and vituperative at this point, she wondered out loud whether Mother had reason to "beg" for the patient's affection and understanding, never having got her fair share. Mother was loving and generous with Renée and her two younger sisters, but the patient was always treated as if she were mature beyond her years. Mother tried to use her as a confidante, and Renée resented this; she felt she was too important to her mother.

I now had a technical problem to think about: to let her go on, simply complaining about her parents until some clues materialized about where I might profitably intervene, was a luxury that I could not afford, given the limited time in which I had to work. Even if she was right about her impressions of her childhood, how would complaining about her parents let her deal more effectively with her present situation? Sometimes, of course, it is very important to listen patiently to just such feelings. For the person who has not dared to complain about his or her parents, being freed by the therapeutic situation to become aware of and voice hidden resentments can be subjectively relieving and can also lead to important insights into that person's unconscious. But there was nothing unconscious about Ms. Lobach's complaints—quite the contrary; and simply to let her continue to blame her parents in some global way for her unhappiness, that is, for her incompetence, would not help her resolve her dilemma. Even though there may be a connection between her complaint of a psychologically confused and deprived childhood and her present situation (and who would doubt that there was?), the link between the two was missing.

By focusing on the past, she avoided talking about the present. So I decided to explore that: What was going on in her life besides not being able to study, I wanted to know. She said that she spent most of her time with her friends. I asked her to describe these people and their activities. Although couched in self-serving terms— "I nurture my friends," "they depend on me totally," and "they make me feel guilty that I'm never doing enough for them"—what she described was a situation in which all sorts of troubled, marginal people found in her someone weaker, even more malleable than they themselves were. Her stridently feminist friends insist that she must hate men and are intolerant of her (unrequited) crush on a male neighbor. He, however, is an anti-intellectual, a dropout who spends his time taking drugs and preaching anarchy to like-minded compatriots. He uses her, but despises the patient for remaining in school and, horror of horrors, being a willing member of the armed forces. It turned out that most nights the patient is home alone. All her so-called friends exclude her from their activities but are more than eager the next day to bend her ear with their troubles.

Her remarks illustrate the need to beware of accepting a patient's words at face value. It would have been a mistake to assume that I understood what Ms. Lobach was describing, though we use the same vocabulary. The use of the term *friend* and what she is willing to call *friendship* is quite different from the connotation that I give these terms. The picture I now formed of the patient was of a person so desperate for companionship and affection that she was eager to take on whatever personality a correspondent might need her to assume, only to find herself used and rejected.

We see here a deeper incompetence than the complaint relating to her schoolwork. Evaluating the patient's capacity to meet the needs for kinship, idealization, and validation (mirroring), I saw the patient failing on all three fronts: Her nonrelationship with so-called friends represented a failure of kinship; her seeming rejection of social mores expressed, I thought, a despair about ever finding an idealizable person; and her poor relationship with her parents set a pattern that she could not break. Her appearance and arrogant demeanor would tend to militate against mirroring approval, if my reaction to her was an indicator of how other members of the academic community in which she was trying to function might respond to her. Furthermore, her incompetence appeared to be spread throughout all sectors of development—autonomy, attachment, creativity, and psychosexuality.

It is especially important, when faced with this sort of psychological global disaster, not to neglect the assets or competencies that the patient brings to the therapy. After all, whatever the problems with her upbringing, she had survived and prevailed: going out on her own to make a life in the service (autonomy), apparently relating well enough to others to be promoted (attachment), and pursuing her interests in such a manner as to be selected for special training (creativity). Ms. Lobach's history of achievement gave me hope.

I was now in a position to become empathic with her communications. No longer in the grip of my affective reaction to her appearance and demeanor, I was able to substitute the affect of interest for the initial contempt I had felt when I first met her. In stepping back from my immediate reaction to the patient's appearance and demeanor and thinking about her situation in developmental terms, I had been able to restore the appropriate therapeutic equanimity to which every patient is entitled—accepting the manner in which she presented herself as an important piece of information rather than as a personal insult. I was now ready to formulate hypotheses that could be tested against the clinical material as it emerged.

I should add that my change in attitude, from anxious puzzlement and a readiness to reject the patient, to one of willingness to be her therapist and try to figure out what was going on and how I might help her, undoubtedly resulted in changes of my bodily posture, my tone of voice, and even my choice of words. In this way, I conveyed on the affective level to Ms. Lobach that her need for kinship had been met; she was no longer a stranger or outsider for me, but instead, we now shared complementary roles in a system being forged by the two of us.

During the interview, Ms. Lobach dealt with the rejection by her friends by rationalizing their behavior with bravado and braggadocio: her friends were in awe of her; she was too much to handle; that's the reason they could be with her for only short periods of time and in a one-on-one situation. Her sadness breaking through for a moment, she said that she had introduced many people to each other and that she was a great matchmaker; but there seemed to be no one for her. "They seem so sure of who they are," she said wistfully. "And you are not?" I asked rhetorically She said that she thought she had had a good idea of who she was and where she wanted to go, but now she seems to have no direction. What she had wanted to achieve makes no sense to her any more. I noted to myself, however, that her avowed reason for coming to see me was precisely to get help in making her scholastic mark and winning her new post: so it isn't all meaningless.

I thought I could now see some connection between her complaints about her parents and what was presently going on in her life. Instead of guiding her, her parents may well have mistaken her precocious intellect for maturity and involved her in their quarrels and dissatisfactions. Now, as a young adult, she is still looking for guidance—that is, an appropriate idealizing selfobject experience—but does not know how to get it. She seems to be limited to dealing defensively with her need by sneering at, and rejecting dependence on, legitimate authority while trying to promote kinship experiences to make up for her lack of idealizable figures. This fails because she chooses unsuitable companions for mutual selfobject support, repeating with them the patterns that her parents established—that is, an inappropriate relationship in which she serves the needs of others and is herself left unrequited.

I thought to myself that probably her transition from the organized, orienting milieu provided by the army to the confusing, free-wheeling atmosphere of a university, which leaves each student to find his or her own way, had been more than Renée could tolerate. What to do? I decided to eliminate the search for insight in favor of crisis intervention and short-term problem-oriented goals. Rather than permitting the origin of her difficulties to unfold over time, I chose to address their consequences: that is, under stress the patient had lost the capacity to organize her experience. Because orientation to her situation and her place in it—the domain of the emergent self—had suffered, I thought I would address that issue first.

I now needed to determine whether the patient had the developmental leeway to improve her situation, given appropriate opportunities for heretofore missing selfobject experiences. In my opinion, her most striking selfobject need was idealization: she needed something or someone to believe in in order to reorient herself, to decide who she was and where she was going. Could she transfer her idealizing need to me and rely on me, rather than on her so-called friends, for problem solving? Would I be able to serve the function of the good parent—the effective parent she never had? Or is every parental figure too contaminated by past empathic failures? How to meet what I considered her idealizing needs? Looking at the developmental spiral, should I attempt to deal with self-esteem issues directly? She already has a nonfunctional, exaggerated sense of self-importance. There is no point in attacking that defense head-on: It won't do anything except increase resistance; trying to bolster genuine self-esteem is pointless in the face of her present acknowledged global incompetence.

Shall I address behavior? A definite possibility. More preferable would be entering the developmental spiral at the level of decision making. This would give her more sense of participation and growth, perhaps even permitting me to help her understand how she makes decisions about her behavior and what the patterns of expectation are that influence her. Although helping her devise behavioral strategies would indirectly meet her need for an idealized other's input, such an approach might increase dependence beyond what is desirable, given our limited opportunity to work together in therapy. Whether I would have to fall back, after all, on that strategy would depend on whether the patient was already too depressed to participate on the decision-making level.

Though the patient described herself as anxious, in my scheme of things (Basch 1988) her situation was more serious. I think of anxiety as the system reaction of the brain to the failure of reflection—anxiety mobilizing the individual's resources in an all-out effort to deal with a perceived threat to the brain's ordering function. Ms. Lobach, however, seems to have gone beyond that to the phase of helplessness called depression. Her inability to concentrate, not getting up in the morning, difficulty making even simple decisions, and lack of productivity suggest as much. On the other hand, her ability to come and seek help, and her forceful personality, even though the latter struck me as overbearing and unpleasant, are assets that show she has not yet retreated completely—she still has some hope. If, however, intervention at the decision-making level is ineffective, then one can always fall back on behavioral intervention. (For treating a depression by entering the developmental spiral at the behavioral level, see my example of Dr. Osgood [Basch 1988, pp. 30–36].)

Accordingly, in an effort to focus on her decision-making process, I said to her that it seemed to me that she had relinquished her right to lead her life as she might see fit, apparently having decided that she had to meet others' needs and subordinate herself to their agenda. Was this really the price one had to pay for friendship? If so, was it worth it? Would she lose every one of her friends if she did not behave in such an accommodating manner? I did not question the validity of her so-called friendships, or point out how she was being used, or how the need to accommodate matched what seems to have gone on with her mother. I focused only on the decision-making function as such.

Ms. Lobach did not say much more than she had not thought about her situation in that way. Her face lost its tenseness, however, and assumed a pensive expression. So ended our first meeting.

When I saw her again a few days later, she said that she had been in an unusually calm and good mood. I then related her improvement to

our work in the therapeutic session, implicitly acknowledging her idealizing need and its legitimacy by calling attention to the part I was
playing in her life. I thought, based on her ready response to my
intervention in the first session, that behind her arrogance was a deep
sense of humiliation concerning her needs. By treating the importance
of my intervention openly and as a matter of course, I hoped to head
off a reaction of shame for needing my help. She said, "My parents never
taught me how to live. They were progressive and were always afraid
that they would be dictating to me, imposing themselves on me by
offering guidance. I think they were just unsure themselves of what was
right." She was indirectly telling me that it was not so much what I said,
but rather, that it was my attitude—my willingness to take an active
lead in the session instead of sitting by passively and expecting her to
carry the ball—that made a difference.

I pointed out how, developmentally speaking, parents who are unsure
of what is best for a child leave that child in a quandary; children depend
on their parents' guidance to tell them what the world is like; later they
can rebel against that all they want. Paradoxically, it is the earlier
security of being able to rely on one's parents' views that makes it safe
to differ later and go one's own way.

With this intervention I validated her need for a supportive relationship by pointing out that it is a normal, necessary aspect of development. In doing so, I reasoned that, kinship and idealization needs having
been met, she was now ready for the mirroring, or validating, input that
prepares a person to stand on her own.

Initially, all three selfobject needs were significantly impaired. As I
recounted, I dealt with the kinship issue by conveying to her that I saw
her as a person whose problems could potentially be understood, and
I dealt with her idealizing need by my willingness to organize her
thinking about her situation. On the basis of my earlier intervention, she
was now in a position to accept validation for the effective moves she
was making. Had I attempted to mirror her initially with comments such
as, "Well, I can see where you are a very troubled person," or, "I can
appreciate how difficult all this must be for you," I would expect that
despite whatever immediate comfort she might have derived from them,
my comments would have had no lasting effect on her attempt to
reorganize her life.

Ms. Lobach said that she had been a withdrawn child until she entered

173

grammar school. At that time, she started to have many friends and became a leader. "I let others live off me," she said. In this session she showed that she had more insight into her behavior than she had initially indicated. She is quite aware of how much she wants to have a relationship with a man but has to pretend that she doesn't care when the others walk away with men in whom she is interested.

In this second session, the patient answered the question of whether I was dealing with a simple decompensation in competence, or a regression, that is, a loss of skills and an inability to function as an adult. Ms. Lobach's integration in response to my intervention in the initial session reassured me that there had been no loss of cognitive or affective capacity. This increased the probability that she could be helped fairly quickly, at least with her immediate problem. Had she been incapable of operating in an age-appropriate manner, that limitation might well have precluded such a therapeutic approach.

In her third session, Ms. Lobach's appearance was much improved; she seemed well put together, cleaner, and neater. She said that she was feeling very different—more energetic—and was reading once again. She can now remember why she originally chose her field of study and how much she enjoys it. She finds that she does not have to call people she does not want to talk to.

"Do I have to love my parents?" she wanted to know, and told me more about her parents' lives. They seem to be well meaning but very confused people, was my conclusion, which I imparted to her. I said, "The issue is not one of loving or not loving; it is the problem of still being very much attached to people who cannot help you in certain respects. You are learning now that you can rely on yourself both to think things through and, when needed, find appropriate help." I was again modulating the idealizing transference, not undermining it, but leavening it with a mirroring (validating) response directed toward autonomy and the domain of the core self. She was building genuine self-esteem based on competent behavior, which I acknowledged.

In her next-to-last visit she came in saying that she was preparing for her exams and feeling quite confident that she would have no trouble. We talked about her future plans, and I suggested that if she needed to do so, she could keep in touch with me by phone. At this she bristled. I had apparently failed her empathically with my well-meant suggestion. She would never have come here, she said, if it had not been a short-term situation. She had no intention of becoming dependent on me. Rather lamely, I explained that I was only trying to tell her that if parting presented problems or if new problems arose, it helps some patients to know they can be in touch, but I was certainly willing to accept her decision that this was not her situation. With some of her old acerbity, she said that if she wanted to get in touch with me she could pick up the phone and did not need an invitation. "Very true," I said.

This exchange shamed me. I made my offer, expecting a positive, or at least neutral, response; instead I was chastised. Unlike infants or children who experience the raw *affect* of shame, however, and for a greater or lesser time experience themselves as totally worthless, I suffered the limited and not so global *emotion* of shame—painful, but much less devastating (Basch, 1988). I felt misunderstood and was aware of being rejected, that is, of being made to feel that there was something wrong with me. But I was able to make a quick recovery. I forgave myself for my blunder and thought I understood why she had to reject my well-meant offer: her need for a dependable idealizing relationship had been met, but now it had to be given up. And because it was still very much connected to early attachment needs, how could a long-distance connection substitute for our being together? If my assumption was correct, then her contempt might well be a reaction to the fear she felt as she doubted my ability to help her deal with the reality of our separation.

To the degree I was successful in stepping back from my emotional reaction and using it to understand the unspoken message Ms. Lobach was trying to send me, I attained empathic understanding, the final transformation of affect—the ability to accept another's affect on his or her terms.

Had I been subject only to the affect of shame per se, I would have been seized by it, unable to think about Ms. Lobach's situation out of a need to protect myself, and for a longer or shorter time would have been lost to the patient. In retrospect, I was, however, more humbled than I realized at the time. Though I managed the grace to acknowledge the correctness of her reprimand, I did not then think about and explore with her the possibility that in my offer for continued contact she may have sensed a difficulty in my giving her up: a repetition of her parents' need for her that caused her to become frightened and to lash out. Shame blocks for a time the capacity to use one's mature cognitive potential. Shame reduces us, to some extent, to the helplessness of infancy; once again we experience a threat to the cohesiveness of the self, a danger whose quality and intensity is like no other.

For her last session, Renée wore her uniform—a visibly different person from the one who had come in six weeks previously. She was confident and hopeful. She had received the assignment she wanted and looked forward to her new duties. She thanked me and we parted. I have not heard from her since that time.

In retrospect, it became clear to me that I had misread the import of Ms. Lobach's initial appearance. Rather than, as I thought at the time, communicating contempt, her bedraggled presentation of herself was possibly a plea: a message from the unconscious to disregard her haughty manner, to look behind her arrogant words and see the helpless, woebegone child who needed help.

Although I have not heard again from Ms. Lobach and do not know how she has used her therapeutic experience, I have had the opportunity to follow enough patients to learn that what seemed to be very simple, or even simplistic, interventions often have had long-lasting and far-reaching results—results that I would not hesitate to label change in psychic structure. It helps, of course, when fate is kind and cooperates by letting the patient use to advantage what he or she has learned and experienced in therapy.

## Guilt or Anger? Robert Candel

Mr. Robert Candel, a forty-five-year-old widower, a research chemist by profession, was referred by his internist for treatment of extreme anxiety and confusion. He presented himself in the initial session very much as his family doctor described—distraught, agitated, and almost tearful. It took some minutes before he could speak. When he was able to quiet down, he told me something of his past history.

Mr. Candel had been married at the age of twenty, and shortly after he and his bride returned from their honeymoon they were in a very serious automobile accident. Telling me this, the patient began to cry hard. He was driving after he had had some drinks, but he did not think at that time that he was intoxicated. As far as the police and the insurance investigator were concerned, he was not at fault in what happened; nonetheless, he was never able to rid himself completely of feeling blame for the seriously crippling injuries that his wife suffered. Although she lived for another twenty years, his wife was permanently paralyzed below the waist and required constant care, which he devotedly gave to her.

She died five years before the time the patient saw me. At the time of her death, Mr. Candel was aware only of feeling exhausted by the strain of caring for her while also carrying on a very busy, successful professional life that generated the kind of money he needed to make his wife's existence as comfortable as it could be—special equipment, nursing care during the day when he was gone, and so on. When he came home, he would take over, and he cared for her not only physically but psychologically. He said he could not remember in those twenty years one night in which he slept uninterruptedly: her physical pain and psychological distress required him to minister to her frequently.

During those years, he felt devoted to his wife and was a man of strong principles, which he attributed to the teachings of his missionary parents. It was this sense of obligation that would have made it inconceivable for him to behave in any way other than he did: he was always surprised when people who learned of his situation commended him and/or praised him for his dedication.

For the first few years after his wife's death, the patient avoided all opportunities for relationships with women. After what he had been through, he did not want to take the chance that fate would once again devastate him. He just wanted to be left alone to mourn, not so much for his wife, but for the youth that he had been and the years that had been lost to both of them. He felt prematurely old and worn out, and he thinks that he was probably depressed.

Two years ago he met a lively twenty-five-year-old woman, Dorothy, at a friend's home. They got along very well and he began to date her. He found that Dorothy's personality brought him out of his despondent mood, and he began to think that maybe he did have another chance at a better life. In due time they became sexually involved and talked of living together—perhaps one day getting married. And, indeed, Dorothy did move into his home a few months before his present upset started. Once she was living with him, he found himself sexually impotent and became increasingly upset and disturbed: he had failed a woman once again and felt guilty. As far as he was concerned, here he was, at the age of forty-five, an old man, robbing this young person of her chance to have a decent relationship and a fulfilled life.

Though the patient was open with me, and demonstrated no cognitive disability and had an appropriate range of affect, I was not satisfied that I understood what was going on; something was missing from his story. In any case, the patient presented serious, immediate problems. He had described symptoms of sleeplessness, agitation, anorexia, some weight loss—all signs of a possible endogenous, or vegetative, depression. I suggested that we try, in addition to our psychotherapeutic visits, an antidepressant. I had established that he was not suicidal, and since he was functioning well in most areas of his life, at this point he did not seem to need hospitalization. The patient agreed to try the medication. When he came back a few days later for his second appointment, however, he complained of side effects and said that he had decided to discontinue the pills, and he wondered what he should do now. I suggested that we keep on talking about his situation and learn what we could.

The patient then spoke once again about what a big disappointment he was to Dorothy, and how unfair this was to her. I asked him how Dorothy felt about it all. "What was her reaction?" I wanted to know. Well, she was very angry, he said. "She feels trapped." He began to talk more about her demanding nature and he mentioned, in an aside, that right from the beginning of their association, she had made it very clear that she was an independent spirit, and that their relationship was not in any way to hamper or tie her down. Specifically, she claimed to have a platonic friendship with a young male colleague of hers, whom she insisted on seeing for extended periods several times a week. And it seemed to me from the way he spoke, though he did not come out with it directly, that my patient was afraid that this association, if it was not so already, would become a sexual one.

Almost as an afterthought, he let me know that Dorothy was quite demanding. She expected Mr. Candel to support her. Because she had previously been living in an apartment near to this other man's house and had now moved in with Mr. Candel, she wanted him to buy her an automobile, so that she could more easily commute to see this other man. "Well, how do you feel about this?" I asked. Again he talked about his distress and anxiety, continuing to blame himself for hurting Dorothy and making her life miserable.

I now experienced myself momentarily drifting off into a reverie about Dorothy and her young lover in bed (as far as I was concerned, they were undoubtedly sexually involved), laughing at my patient and planning the next indignity they would visit upon him. I pulled myself out of this fantasy and took the first step toward establishing empathy with what Mr. Candel had just told me (figure 5.2); namely, I realized that I was very angry at this woman.

The question now was whether in my anger I was resonating with Mr. Candel's unspoken affect, or whether I was responding affectively to how I would feel if I were in his situation. I studied Mr. Candel's tone of voice, facial expression, and posture. I also looked for other autonomically generated signs of affect that were not finding conscious expression in the form of feeling. I did not detect any such markers. Had they been present, I would have found myself the target of so-called projective identification (Ogden 1979): a situation in which the patient subtly causes the therapist to resonate autonomically with the patient's unconscious affect-laden fantasies, which can then eventually be made conscious for, and more acceptable to, the patient. I concluded that my reaction was my own, a response to how I would have experienced Dorothy's demands.

This process of self-examination enabled me to establish that Mr. Candel really felt no anger, but instead, felt guilty that he, through his impotence, was letting Dorothy down.

What to do? Taking the next step in utilizing empathic understanding, I thought that perhaps the guilt he felt toward his late wife had spread to his present relationship, so that he could not think about his present situation in other terms and become aware of the resentment he might be expected to feel under the circumstances. I did not believe that a massive disavowal of affect generally, or anger in particular, was involved, for I had ascertained during the first session that he had a reasonable range of emotions, and was no stranger to angry feelings. I decided to broach the subject with him, and, accordingly, wondered out loud whether, perhaps, he was angry that Dorothy insisted on maintaining her liaison with this man. He pondered my question and concluded that he had not felt anger in relation to this situation; it seemed that what I had said was of interest to him intellectually only.

When he came back for his third session, he said he had been sleeping much better and was no longer impotent. Mr. Candel was quite clear as to how this had come to pass: "What you said last time absolutely made the difference. When I left here I began to think more about it. I had reversed cause and effect: my impotence was not the cause of the problem, but the result of the problem, namely, her behavior. I think I am a little angry at her but, I think, more amazed that I let this happen to me. How could I not have seen what was going on? Now that I understand it, I am back in charge. I haven't decided exactly what to do, but I know I can handle it."

It seemed that Mr. Candel had quickly transferred his need for an idealizable authority to me, and in that context my comment had permitted him to reorient himself to his situation and to think clearly about his relationship with Dorothy. The restoration of his sense of competence was indicated both by his statement, "I'm back in charge . . . ," and by his emotional reaction. He did not fly into a rage at Dorothy. Genuine insight is usually accompanied, as it was here, by a sense of wonderment at how one's decision making was affected by past patterns of operation: The patient's affect is directed inward, not outward.

As I said, I do not think that the defense of disavowal of affect was involved directly in his inability to come to grips with his relationship to Dorothy. Unconscious defenses are not lifted so readily, no matter how accurate a therapist's interpretation may be. In Mr. Candel's case the problem seems to have resided in the cognitive arm of the thought process (Basch 1988, p. 81, figure 4.3). The incoming data relating to Dorothy's behavior was integrated by Mr. Candel in keeping with the guilt-laden pattern of expectation that had evolved in his relationship with his late wife. He automatically saw himself at fault for whatever problems arose in a relationship with a woman: he unconsciously assumed that he was guilty and had to atone. My intervention apparently opened that closed system and permitted him to reevaluate the situation with Dorothy as Dorothy, and he no longer experienced her only as a surrogate for his late wife. We are used to working so hard and over a long period of time with our patients to achieve such a far-reaching result, that when something clicks so early and so easily, as it did with Mr. Candel, I, for one, was suspicious of the validity and stability of what had happened. Of course, I kept those reservations to myself.

In the patient's fourth session, he began to tell me that he had come to some conclusions and had made certain decisions. He realized that much as he liked Dorothy and thought that she cared for him too, he could not tolerate this situation. He contrasted it to the life he had led before, one in which he and his injured spouse had formed an inseparable unit. Now there was an atmosphere in which the strength of the union between himself and Dorothy was always in question: "Does she care for me, doesn't she care for me? Does she care more for this other man? She is younger; what if she gets tired of me? When she is forty or so, I'll be sixty-five; what is going to happen to us then?" This kind of self-imposed tension, he concluded, was no longer tolerable. He had a talk with Dorothy and told her that neither living together nor marrying her in the future were things that he felt particularly comfortable with at this time. He also confronted her for the first time, firmly but not angrily, with the unfairness of her various demands upon him, especially material ones. He then made it clear to her that he felt he had been more than generous and that he was not going to continue to support her. There were some bills that he had agreed to pay, and he said he would honor that promise; but once that was done, they could, if she wanted to, renegotiate the relationship. What might happen then was something he could not predict.

Inwardly, I could not but agree with what the patient told me. He was reasonable and clearly was attempting to be fair to both himself and his now ex-lover. Nothing in his tone, demeanor, or appearance indicated anything other than the calm, reasonable resolve that he had expressed. What I would have then liked to do was to continue therapy with him, exploring more thoroughly the relationship with his late wife. Given his devotion to her, it would not have been unexpected that over all those years of her invalidism, anger would have come up. How had the negative feelings about his situation been dealt with, and, if they were there, how might they be prevented from detracting from future relationships? Was there on a deeper level a disavowal of affect in some sector, or some aspect of a sector, of his development that needed to be further examined? I made some comments indicating that we should continue to explore his situation, but he was quite satisfied with what he had achieved. He said that he now felt fine, was able to function, and thought that he would discontinue therapy. He expressed his gratitude and, with some amazement, compared himself to the way he had been just a few short weeks ago. He did say that if he got into difficulties in the future, he would like to see me again, which I, of course, readily agreed to do. At the end of the session he thanked me once more; we shook hands and parted. I have not heard from him since, and assume that he has been doing well.

## A Case of Pseudo-Paranoia: Merrill Sherman

With his horn-rim glasses and his tweed suit, Merrill Sherman looked very much the academic that he was. "My wife says I'm driving her crazy," was how he opened our meeting. "I know she's right, but I've got to talk to somebody about it. When she couldn't stand it anymore she sent me here to talk to you; I don't know what a psychiatrist can do about it; for me, it's a moral issue."

What troubled Mr. Sherman, a thirty-four-year-old assistant dean at an out-of-town university, was the reprehensible conduct of his chief, Dean Ballard. Mr. Sherman outlined clearly and in detail what made him so indignant. Dean Ballard rode roughshod over the ideas of the professors and administrators under him. He took advantage of his position by coming late and leaving early when he chose to do so, while insisting that all others adhere to their respective schedules. On several occasions, when entertaining at departmental expense, the Ballards had guests whose relation to university business was questionable. On trips for the university, the dean often tacked on a day or two for his private amusement. Mr. Sherman had obtained the dean's automobile mileage records so as to establish whether the university car assigned to him was being used strictly for business. My patient suspected that it was not, for he had seen Mrs. Ballard come out of that automobile with packages, indicative of a shopping trip to a downtown department store.

More and more of Mr. Sherman's days—and nights—were being taken up by his vendetta. He simply could not think or talk of anything else. He was now scheming to go to some members of the board of trustees, who, he knew, were not enamored of the man, to see if they would use his evidence to bring proceedings against Dean Ballard and have him dismissed.

As I listened to Mr. Sherman, I found myself becoming increasingly uncomfortable. I evaluated what he was saying in terms of my past experience, direct and vicarious, with various administrative hierarchies and concluded that he was headed for trouble. What to him were terrible failings in his superior hardly sounded like the sorts of things that would get a person in high office dismissed from his post; indeed, many might feel that what Mr. Sherman seemed to find so terribly dishonest were the unwritten perquisites of rank. I very much doubted that Mr. Sherman's quest would result in anyone's downfall but his own.

I wondered for a while whether Mr. Sherman was suffering from a monosymptomatic paranoid psychosis, but it didn't "feel" that way. He displayed no thought disorder, his affect was appropriate, and he in no way felt persecuted by Dean Ballard. For him, as he said, the dean's behavior was morally offensive and he felt obligated to root it out. He felt he owed it to the university to bring the miscreant to justice.

What should my next step be? Point out to the patient the danger he was running by his behavior? He could easily find himself out of a job and his future in academia ruined if word about his activities got out—and that would very likely happen if he started to talk to members of the board of trustees. Or should I try to impose on Mr. Sherman my view of the reality of how bureaucracies work? Given the intensity with which he presented his convictions, the first course would be useless, the second impossible. In any case, that my view of his situation differed from his was not without significance, but, for the moment at least, it did not belong in the patient's treatment. I consciously avoided premature closure, so that I could continue to listen, explore, and learn more about the patient's view of reality.

Mr. Sherman was seemingly oblivious to the consequences he was courting by his behavior. His perceived failure of competence—what frustrated him and made him feel helpless—lay in his wife's refusal to listen to him any longer. As he said, "I have to talk to someone about it." Since that was clearly where his affect was, when he had exhausted his store of grievances against Dean Ballard and looked to me for direction, I did not say, "Just go on and tell me whatever occurs to you," or "Tell me some other things about yourself." Instead, focusing on his need to talk about his preoccupation with the dean's conduct, and his frustration when he wasn't listened to or taken seriously, I asked him to give me more details about the university hierarchy—who was who and where he or she fit in. As he elaborated, I got a very good picture of the broader context in which the patient worked. I learned a great deal about how he had come to choose this career and how he was functioning when not pursuing the dean. In all other areas, he was operating admirably; he showed himself to be a perfectly pleasant person whose abilities had been widely recognized and had won him rapid advancement. I also learned that Mr. Sherman's all-consuming concern had begun shortly after a friend and colleague had left to take a position at another university. This man shared Mr. Sherman's low opinion of their chief, and they would talk frequently about Dean Ballard's opportunistic behavior and what a bad example he was setting for everyone else.

It was important to me that I had a picture of what was "right" with the patient. As we came to the end of our first session, I felt reassured by the history of his successful quest for competence in the workplace but remained puzzled by the intensity of his moral outrage. His inability to contain his concern in a (by my standards) reasonable fashion led me to think that something was going on psychologically that needed to be understood—but what might that be? I thought I had one clue that could prove to be helpful. He had mentioned that his disdain for Dean Ballard had been translated into action after his colleague and confidant left the university. I wondered if his friend's departure had undermined his kinship needs and whether his rage was a displaced reaction to the disorientation and sense of deprivation that this loss precipitated.

I had wanted to see Mr. Sherman more frequently, but he said that the three-hour trip to my office meant he could come only once a week, and since he did not seem in danger of drastic decompensation, I agreed to see him on that basis. In his second appointment with me, he apologized and laughed at himself for having nothing new to talk about: all that was on his mind was the situation with the dean. I thought to myself that he might be worrying that, like his wife, I would tire of his obsessive concern. I suggested he go right ahead; since the situation with the dean was what was most disturbing to him, it was not surprising that that was what he was impelled to talk about.

Mr. Sherman again launched into a bitter description of what the dean had been doing, how he despised that sort of behavior, and so on. What was different, however, was that this time he himself began to wonder at his behavior. He knew very well that the majority's attitude toward the dean would most likely be RHIP (rank has its privileges). He was also very much aware of the risk he was running and had been warned by various colleagues, as well as by his wife, that he would be the loser in any open contest with his chief. (Silently, I congratulated myself for having kept quiet about what was obvious.) Yet, he said, he could not help himself, could not just forget about it or moderate himself. He had been toying with the idea of quitting his job, but he liked his work and felt he did not want to give up what he had earned and the opportunities that awaited him. The connections he had built up and the reputation he had gained put him in line for some good promotions; indeed some other institutions had already sounded him out to see if he might want to make a move to a higher position. All this could be lost, he knew, if he pursued his vengeful course; nevertheless, he was prepared to forge ahead. He planned to talk to one of the like-minded trustees he had mentioned to me, when that person returned from vacation some weeks hence.

Again, I did not come down on the side of his "rational self" and try to dissuade him from his plan. I was glad to hear, however, that we had at least some time before he could talk to his friend on the board. What I did say was that when we find a patient in a situation like his—namely, experiencing a strong pull in one direction, while another part of his mind is questioning, but cannot prevent him from doing what he is doing—then that is a clear indication that there is more going on than meets the eye. The program that is running itself out may also be meeting some needs not immediately apparent. I hastened to add that I had no ideas about what that underlying motivation might be, only that what he had said pointed toward work that we should do together. Whatever thoughts I had about the possibility that, in spite of everything I had learned, Mr. Sherman might still be psychotic were dispelled when he let me know that, though he could not alter them, he could step back from his beliefs and judge them according to customary standards.

Mr. Sherman began his third appointment by saying, "Now let's start on the rest of me." He then proceeded to talk about his childhood and adolescence. He was the only child of his mother. His father was a widower twenty years older than she with four children. Two older girls were already grown and out of the house when the patient was born, but he grew up with his two stepbrothers, one six and the other eight years older than my patient. The father was not unkind, but he was a stern disciplinarian. He owned the bank in the small town in which they lived, and he was very concerned with proper appearance and conduct. Father felt that it was incumbent upon him in his position to set an example for others, and he expected his family to do the same. Strict standards for mannerly behavior were set, and the need for high achievement in school and community activities was stressed. Merrill learned very early the advantages brought by conformity; he was clearly the favorite of his mother, who always told him that she was so grateful that she could count on him to satisfy his father and keep peace in the house. Father was not pleased with the men his daughters had married, and his chronic irritability about this translated into extra vigilance to ensure his sons did not fall by the wayside. Neither of the patient's stepbrothers lived up to father's expectations. Ralph, the one next in age to Merrill, was constantly rebelling against his father and arousing the latter's wrath. As long as Merrill could remember, he dreaded the altercations between father and Ralph, both of whom Merrill loved very much. He would sit, inwardly terrified as the daily argument between the two got started, thinking to himself, "No, Ralphy, no—don't say that, say so-and-so." But Ralph, in spite of Merrill's attempts to coach him privately, would invariably say or do the exact thing that would throw his father into a despairing rage. At those times the atmosphere in the house grew tense, with mother crying and the two older boys sulking, until someone, usually Merrill, was able to please father and temporarily generate a better mood.

Merrill liked school, and, as he got older, would spend as much time after school as he could reading in the library, hiking in the nearby woods, bicycling or, in the winter, cross-country skiing. These were activities that he could engage in alone, they were approved of by father; and, most important, their pursuit took him away from his tension-filled home. As the patient told me this, he found himself crying uncontrollably for a few minutes. When he recovered his composure, he went on to say that he felt terribly guilty that he seldom, if ever, was punished, while Ralph and his other brother were always being deprived of privileges or assigned extra duties by his father. He became tearful as he recalled how often he would want to cry out to his father, "Leave Ralph alone," and to his brother, "God, Ralphy, don't make it worse." He wanted someone to step in and stop the eternal wrangling. Often he would feel like saying, "Pick on me, he's no worse than I am." He ended up getting a lot more from his parents, both emotionally and materially, than either of his brothers. "Perhaps," I said, "this is one factor in your strong feelings about Dean Ballard. Here is someone who is getting more than what's fair and, far from feeling guilty about it, seems to glory in his privileged position." He heard me and was thoughtful, and then went on recounting his childhood history.

As Merrill grew up, his interest in reading led him to history and eventually to an academic career. Although he liked teaching, he soon found that, even though only an instructor and then an assistant professor, his ability to negotiate and reconcile differing points of view between faculty members brought him into demand as a representative on various university committees. He seemed, as he said, to be able to take others' positions into consideration and find solutions to problems that reasonably satisfied all sides. "That expertise you brought from home," I said.

While still a graduate student, Mr. Sherman met his wife, who was then a medical student. Their marriage has been a comfortable one, he said. Both are satisfied with their respective careers and they have a wide circle of friends. Neither one wants children and they are free to travel, which both enjoy. Yet, Mr. Sherman said, there is something missing for him. Lately he finds himself looking at other women, though he hasn't done anything about his desires. "What is the nature of those wishes; what are your fantasies?" I wanted to know. Mostly of being held and caressed, he told me; though his wife is a good sexual partner, he often does not feel loved enough by her.

In retrospect, I think I was correct in my hypothesis that Mr. Sherman's overreaction to his chief's behavior had been precipitated by his colleague's leaving. Perhaps it is not too far-fetched to think that he and his friend had formed a brotherly kinship bond that made it possible to cope with the dean/father. I wish I had addressed that issue instead of trying out the interpretation that had Mr. Sherman angry at Dean Ballard because the patient was reliving guilt vis-à-vis his brother Ralph. Once his friend had left, his attempt to restore the kinship bond through discussion with his wife failed; the patient became increasingly insistent the more she pulled back from serving that selfobject function for him. My listening to him, and clearly wanting to understand the details of his concern, restored the kinship bond, and that permitted the patient to regain his usual adaptation. His indignation at the dean remained strong, but his manner of dealing with it had none of the desperation fueled by intrapsychic stress. That he spontaneously talked about his early life and its problems heralded, I thought, his belief that I could and would understand him, as well as the hope that I might help him with other than the immediate problems—the beginning of transferring an idealizing need to me.

In a subsequent session, Mr. Sherman volunteered that he had become more "philosophical"; that is, he was more able to look at his frustration with the dean's behavior as a psychological issue and found himself less interested in arranging for the latter's punishment. The patient no longer spent much time in the hour talking about the dean but focused increasingly on his personal life. As he reviewed his history, he spoke of a time shortly after he graduated from his doctoral program, when he and his wife were traveling with a fast crowd. There was an awful lot of drinking, and when all were pretty well soused they would go skinny-dipping. He luxuriated in the sensation of diving naked into the pool and running around nude afterward. Seeing the others naked was not particularly titillating for him; what he enjoyed was being seen. Strangely, he said, he never felt any embarrassment, though usually he is more on the "up-tight" side where manners and decorum are concerned. I said that he seemed to delight in his nudity, very much as a little boy might do—a joy at being accepted for one's self. His inhibitions loosened by alcohol, he could indulge himself in ways he ordinarily could not permit himself.

This led Mr. Sherman to reminisce about the early days of his marriage when his wife, who had attended an osteopathic school of medicine, would practice on him various techniques she had learned for dealing with muscle tension. He enjoyed these manipulations tremendously. Now it seems they have become so distant from one another, that he hesitates even to ask her to scratch his back when they are in bed at night. He misses the touching/tenderness they used to show one another.

I suggested that he had paid a price for his favored position in the family. Always alert for what his parents wanted from him, he neglected his own needs; he soothed his parents when he needed soothing himself. This seemed to make a lot of sense to the patient. He recalled several incidents in which he tried to approach his mother so as to talk to her about his upset with father, only to have her praise him for being so good, and then telling him her troubles. "Yes," I said, "when your wife massaged you and scratched your back, you had a chance to be the little boy you couldn't be then. Perhaps the interest in other women, as your fantasies also suggest, is not so much a quest for sexual excitement as

for the 'babying' that you had for a while in your marriage that somehow got lost."

In the tenth session he returned to his original concern. He is resigned
to the fact that he probably cannot bring the dean to heel, and that
recognition no longer makes him frantic. "Perhaps the dean is the
indulged baby that you wanted to be," I said. "If you can't have special
treatment, then no one should." Mr. Sherman said that his wife was very
pleased that he no longer importuned her with tales of the dean's
behavior. The improved relationship between them let him talk to her
about his need for physical intimacy apart from, or in addition to, sexual
intercourse, and she was quite receptive to that. Now he can understand
why he needs to be babied and can deal with it rationally.

After several more sessions, the patient found himself in good psychological balance; his relationship with his wife continued to improve,
and he was no longer unduly preoccupied with the dean's conduct. He
said he had decided that he had gotten what he wanted from therapy.
He realized, he said, from our discussions, that a lot more could be talked
about, but the trip to Chicago was a long one and, under the circumstances, he would stop. We then terminated with the understanding that
should he want to come to see me in the future, the door was open.

In the patients selected for this section on short-term or time-limited
therapy, there was no barrier to forming an idealizing transference. All
responded positively to the introduction into their lives of what they
implicitly accepted as a benign authority. Relieved and strengthened by
my quasi-parental presence, each of these patients could be helped to
make the most of his or her resources. What surprised me as I reviewed
what I had written was that, with the exception of Mr. Sherman, the
improvement was focused in the developmental sector of autonomy. In
restoring their ability to function once more as centers of initiative
(Kohut 1971), Mr. Lavelle, Ms. Lobach, and Mr. Candel not only took
control of their lives but resolved secondary issues in the sectors of
attachment, psychosexuality, and creativity. As I look back on my
practice, this pattern does seem to hold.

In Mr. Sherman's case it is true that an attachment need was resolved
in a short time, but usually this takes much longer, as do the truly
psychosexual difficulties; the latter, in my experience, usually require
psychoanalysis. Understandably, correcting affective/cognitive deficits

requires time to permit the patient to take successive developmental steps with the support of the appropriate selfobject transferences. As I said, in reviewing my cases, my efforts have had a rapid, definitive effect when the patient's incompetence is localized in the sector of autonomy.

Perhaps this serendipitous clinical finding can be useful in evaluating potential patients whose financial or other logistic constraints limit our therapeutic options. We might be much more willing to accept these limitations if our diagnosis points to issues of autonomy. Also, when I accept a patient who at the outset agrees to come only for short-term treatment, I explicitly or implicitly focus my interventions on autonomy issues and make the most of the clinical opportunity available in that area. This does not mean that other aspects of the patient's difficulties are ignored or not mentioned. Quite the contrary. A frank discussion with the patient of the problems remaining and, if indicated, the need for more extensive treatment is part of terminating short-term therapy. In some cases, the patient may then or later accept the latter recommendation. More often than not, however, the decision is made to live with the unresolved problems, the patient hoping that what has been done will positively influence those other issues over time. Such a confrontation of unresolved difficulties by the patient is, of course, in itself potentially therapeutic.

# *Envoi*

What holds true for our patients also holds true for us, their therapists. We are continuously making and implementing decisions regarding the therapeutic transaction and then evaluating how effective or competent we have been with this interpretation, in that session, in the treatment as a whole. Here, beginning with the basic idea that behind patients' pain is an inability to bring to bear their problem-solving capacities, actual or potential, on the challenges that confront them, I have described what I have found to be critical for an approach geared to clarifying, first for ourselves and then for our patients, what went wrong in their search for competence and self-esteem and, by implication, what they need and might be able to do to relieve their respective difficulties. It is my hope that you, my readers and colleagues, will find that what I have presented and illustrated here can be readily integrated into your work, and that you will experience it as helpful in the search for an empathic understanding of and response to your patients' communications.

# References

Bacal, H. A. (1985). "Optimal responsiveness and the therapeutic process." In A. Goldberg (Ed.). *Progress in self psychology*. Vol. 1 (pp. 202–227). New York: Guilford Press.

Basch, M. F. (1974). "Interference with perceptual transformation in the service of defense." *The Annual of Psychoanalysis, 2,* 87–97.

———— (1975). "Toward a theory that encompasses depression: A revision of existing causal hypotheses in psychoanalysis." In E. J. Anthony & T. Benedek (Eds.). *Depression and Human Existence* (pp. 485–534). Boston: Little, Brown.

———— (1976). "The concept of affect: A re-examination." *Journal of the American Psychoanalytic Association, 24,* 759–777.

———— (1980). *Doing psychotherapy.* New York: Basic Books.

———— (1981). "Psychoanalytic interpretation and cognitive transformation." *International Journal of Psycho-Analysis, 62,* 151–175.

———— (1983a). "Empathic understanding: A review of the concept and some theoretical considerations." *Journal of the American Psychoanalytic Association, 31,* 101–126.

———— (1983b). "The significance of self psychology for a theory of psychotherapy." In J. D. Lichtenberg & S. Kaplan (Eds.). *Reflections on self psychology* (pp. 223–238). Hillsdale, NJ: Analytic Press.

———— (1983c). "The perception of reality and the disavowal of meaning." *The Annual of Psychoanalysis, 11,* 125–154.

———— (1984). "Selfobjects and selfobject transference: Theoretical implications." In P. E. Stepansky & A. Goldberg (Eds.). *Kohut's legacy* (pp. 21–41). Hillsdale, NJ: Analytic Press.

———— (1985). "Interpretation: Toward a developmental model." In A.

Goldberg (Ed.). *Progress in self psychology.* Vol. 1 (pp. 33–42). New York: Guilford Press.

——— (1988). *Understanding psychotherapy: The science behind the art.* New York: Basic Books.

——— (1991). "Selfobject transferences are important in psychotherapy." *Psychiatric Times,* 8(3), 1.

——— (in press). "The significance of a theory of affect for psychoanalytic technique." *Journal of the American Psychoanalytic Association.*

Beebe, B., & Lachmann, F. M. (1988). "Mother-infant mutual influence and precursors of psychic structure. In A. Goldberg (Ed.). *Progress in self psychology.* Vol. 3 (pp. 3–25). Hillsdale, NJ: Analytic Press.

Beebe, B., & Sloate, P. (1982). "Assessment and treatment of difficulties in mother-infant attunement in the first three years of life: A case history." *Psychoanalytic Inquiry, 1,* 601–623.

Beebe, B., & Stern, D. (1977). "Engagement-disengagement and early object experiences." In N. Freedman & S. Grand (Eds.). *Communicative structures and psychic structures* (pp. 35–55). New York: Plenum.

Breuer, J., & Freud, S. (1893–1895). "Studies in hysteria." In *Standard Edition.* Vol. 2. London: Hogarth Press, 1955.

Broucek, F. (1979). "Efficacy in infancy: A review of some experimental studies and their possible implications for clinical theory. *International Journal of Psycho-Analysis, 60,* 311–316.

Burke, J., Jr., White, H., & Havens, L. (1979). "Which short-term therapy? Matching patient and method." *Archives of General Psychiatry, 36,* 177–186.

Detrick, D. W. (1986). "Alterego phenomena and the alterego transferences: Some further considerations." In A. Goldberg (Ed.). *Progress in self psychology.* Vol. 2 (pp. 299–304). New York: Guilford Press.

Field, T. M. (1985). "Neonatal perception of people: Maturational and individual differences." In T. M. Field & N. A. Fox (Eds.). *Social perception in infants* (pp. 31–52). Norwood, NJ: Ahler Publishing.

Firestein, S. K. (1978). *Termination in psychoanalysis.* New York: International Universities Press.

Flegenheimer, W. F. (1982). *Techniques of brief psychotherapy.* New York: Jason Aronson.

Freud, S. (1905). "Three essays on the theory of sexuality." In *Standard Edition.* Vol. 7 (pp. 125–245). London: Hogarth Press, 1953.

——— (1914). "Remembering, repeating and working-through. (Further recommendations on the technique of psycho-analysis II.)" In *Standard Edition.* Vol. 12 (145–146). London: Hogarth Press, 1958.

——— (1915a). "Repression." In *Standard Edition.* Vol. 14 (pp. 141–158). London: Hogarth Press, 1957.

——— (1915b). "The unconscious." In *Standard Edition.* Vol. 14 (pp. 159–204). London: Hogarth Press, 1957.

———— (1915c). "Observations on transference love. (Further recommendations on the technique of psycho-analysis III.)" In *Standard Edition*. Vol. 12 (pp. 157–171). London: Hogarth Press, 1958.

———— (1915–1916). "Introductory lectures on psycho-analysis, Parts I and II." In *Standard Edition*. Vol. 15. London: Hogarth Press, 1963.

———— (1916–1917). "Introductory lectures on psycho-analysis, Part III." In *Standard Edition*. Vol. 16 (pp. 243–476). London: Hogarth Press, 1963.

———— (1923). "The ego and the id." In *Standard Edition*. Vol. 19 (pp. 3–66). London: Hogarth Press, 1961.

———— (1924). "A short account of psycho-analysis." In *Standard Edition*. Vol. 19 (pp. 191–209). London: Hogarth Press, 1961.

———— (1926). "Inhibitions, symptoms and anxiety." In *Standard Edition*. Vol. 20 (pp. 87–179). London: Hogarth Press, 1959.

Goldberg, A. (1973). "Psychotherapy of narcissistic injuries." *Archives of General Psychiatry, 28*, 722–726.

———— (1990). *The prisonhouse of psychoanalysis.* Hillsdale, NJ: Analytic Press.

Gustafson, J. (1984). "An integration of brief dynamic psychotherapy." *American Journal of Psychiatry, 141*, 935–944.

Holinger, P. C. (1989). "A developmental perspective on psychotherapy and psychoanalysis." *American Journal of Psychiatry, 146*, 1404–1412.

Jaffe, C. (1988). "Disavowal: A review of applications in current literature." *The Annual of Psychoanalysis, 16*, 93–110.

Kohut, H. (1971). *The analysis of the self.* New York: International Universities Press.

———— (1977). *The restoration of the self.* New York: International Universities Press.

———— (1984). *How does analysis cure?* Chicago: University of Chicago Press.

Kramer, P. D. (1989). *Moments of engagement.* New York: Norton.

Lichtenberg, J. D. (1989). *Psychoanalysis and motivation.* Hillsdale, NJ: Analytic Press.

Lifton, R. J. (1986). *The Nazi doctors.* New York: Basic Books.

Malcolm, J. (1980, 1981). *Psychoanalysis: The impossible profession.* New York: Alfred A. Knopf.

Nathanson, D. L. (1987). "A timetable for shame." In D. L. Nathanson (Ed.). *The many faces of shame* (pp. 1–63). New York: Guilford Press.

———— (in press). *Shame and pride: Affect, sex, and the birth of the self.* New York: Norton.

Ogden, T. H. (1979). "On projective identification." *International Journal of Psycho-Analysis, 60*, 357–373.

Palombo, J. (1991). "Bridging the chasm between developmental theory and clinical theory. *The Annual of Psychoanalysis, 19*, 151–193.

Piaget, J., & Inhelder, B. (1969). *The psychology of the child.* New York: Basic Books.

Rochlin, G. (1982). "Aggression reconsidered: A critique of psychoanalysis." *Psychoanalytic Inquiry, 2,* 121–132.

Schlessinger, N., & Robbins, F. P. (1983). *A developmental view of the psychoanalytic process.* New York: International Universities Press.

Stern, D. N. (1985). *The interpersonal world of the infant.* New York: Basic Books.

——— (1989). "Crib monologues from a psychoanalytic perspective." In K. Nelson (Ed.). *Narratives from the crib* (pp. 309–319). Cambridge: Harvard University Press.

Strupp, H. (1980a). "Success and failure in time-limited psychotherapy. A systematic comparison of two cases: Comparison 1." *Archives of General Psychiatry, 37* (May), 595–603.

——— (1980b). "Success and failure in time-limited psychotherapy. A systematic comparison of two cases: Comparison 2." *Archives of General Psychiatry, 37* (June), 708–716.

——— (1980c). "Success and failure in time-limited psychotherapy. Further evidence: Comparison 4." *Archives of General Psychiatry, 37* (Aug.), 947–954.

Tomkins, S. S. (1962–1963). *Affect, imagery, consciousness.* Vols. 1 & 2. New York: Springer.

——— (1981). "The quest for primary motives: Biography and autobiography of an idea. *Journal of Personality and Social Psychology, 41,* 306–329.

——— (1987). "Shame." In D. L. Nathanson (Ed.). *The many faces of shame* (pp. 133–161). New York: Guilford Press.

White, R. W. (1959). "Motivation reconsidered: The concept of competence." *Psychological Review, 66,* 297–333.

Winnicott, D. W. (1965). *The maturational processes and the facilitating environment: Studies in the theory of emotional development.* New York: International Universities Press.

# Index

Accommodation, 6, 9

Adolescence: anger in, 106–108, 111–113, 145–148; autonomy in, 97, 104; case study on, 93–114; core self in, 97, 104, 109; emergent self in, 100, 101, 107–108; private self in, 112–113; responsibility in, 95–97, 100, 103–105, 107, 108; self-development in, 97, 98, 100–101, 104, 107, 109, 112–113; self-esteem in, 105; shame in, 104–105; subjective self in, 98, 104, 109

Affect: of children, 2–3; development of, 2–3, 44–45; disavowal of, as defense, 50, 179–181; expression of, 44–45, 63, 64, 108; as guide in therapy, 2–3, 101–103, 108, 118–119; of infants, 2, 3, 67, 70–72; as information source, 2; primacy of, 2–3; projective identification and, 179; in reflex response, 2; of therapist in developing empathy, 87–92, 98

Affect attunement, 37, 51, 136–138

Affect/cognition: as aspect of development, 22, 23; control of, 143–144; shame and, 53–58, 67–69

Affective maturity, 2–3, 6; arrest in, 63, 64, 67–72, 122–124; developmental

spiral and, 10–12; in neurotic patients, 120–121; parenthood and, 67–72

Affect of shame, 176

Aggression, 88–89

Alter ego. See Kinship experience

Analysis. See Psychoanalysis

*Analysis of the Self, The* (Kohut), 59

Anger, 73–92; in adolescence, 106–108, 111–113, 145–148; case study on, 73–92; in childhood, 74–76, 83; empathy in understanding, 87–92; fear of others', 106–108; guilt vs., 176–182; helplessness and, 111–113; of infants, 2; intimacy and, 3–5; toward one's children, 77–78, 85; as plea for help, 81–84, 86, 88; as reaction to anxiety, 44; shame and, 82, 83, 85, 86; toward therapist, 5, 73–74, 78–81, 87–90, 145–148; at work, 74–77, 83

Antidepressant medication, 178

Anxiety, 118–120; anger as reaction to, 44; in defense formation, 27; in formation of idealizing transference, 18, 24–28, 43; nature of, 172; in psychoanalytic approach, 47–50, 119–121

Appreciation, 8